AF415625

Prayers and Bullets

Down in the Dirt
Revealing all your dirty little secrets
March 2021, v181

Assorted artists
scarspublications

Prayers and Bullets

Down in the Dirt

scarspublication

http://scars.tv
Down in the Dirt
March 2021, volume 181
ISSN 1554-9623

Printed in the United States of America,
the United Kingdom, Europe, and Japan

10   9   8   7   6   5   4   3   2   1

Table of Contents

March 2021 Down in the Dirt, v181

Scars Art: 20-22 (photographs of bridges in West Virginia that were photographed ~1994), 64 & 65 (photos of the Senate Square Cathedral, photographed 5/30/06 in Helsinki, Finland), 80 (a replica of a Tank on display in Visakhapatnam, India, photographed 1/15/15), 81 (a replica of a tank photographed in Wisconsin, USA, 9/9/07), 96 (stitches, photographed 9/17/04), 99 (image of Kuypers holding a lit sparkler in front of impromptu artwork from the HA!Man of South Africa that was used for the CD cover and book cover "Burn Through Me", that was also used for the Instagram-Twittr-Tumblr image for the poem "Zircon, Gemstones, Baubles and Bling"), 107 (a photograph is glacial ice collected by John Yotko in the Southern Ocean 11/19/17 near Paradise Harbor in Antarctica, that was used for the Instagram-Twittr-Tumblr image for the poem "Glacial Ice"). Cover art is of graffiti photographed in the French Quarter in New Orleans, LA 11/1/20.

Beak Tug

Nancy May

dune mist
a host of rhinos
speed through willows

Canter Blister

Nancy May

tomato rift
a canary swoops
in a haze of pebbles

Dear Past Self

Adam Cowan

Dear Past Self,

I wish you love,
peace,
and acceptance,
of that which you've known, but felt you needed permission for.

May you know your body better than I did—
How you look into the world,
yet just beyond it,
Eyes full of stories you knew deep down were truth,
Heavy with too many years premature knowledge—
Pain devouring,
fantasy deflecting.

Your hair,
the only part you dare own,
Making yourself known with a silent yet screaming statement,
Reveling inside, unknown to others, when the world mistak-
    enly started calling you 'boy.'
I only wish,
more intentionally,
you would have claimed 'man.'

Man who toils,
creates,
paints,
works,
pushes away— like father—
but afraid to be, knowing your immense sensitivity.

Perhaps it's not bad they think you a woman,
so you can be sensitive without being bothered– like brother–

But couldn't find the spine to declare that truth, that young,
        already burdened by so much no one man
        could handle it.

And so they reside.
And so they comfort.

Leaning on your elbow late at night to listen and ponder the
        messages in your mind,
but somehow beyond.

They speak more truth in silence than one thousand words
        from your kin in the light of day.

And so you walk–your legs strong,
Ever running,
Ever nearing,
Ever searching–
That truth that resides within your own body.

If only then you had known, how different would things be?

But then again, how vastly robbed would be your
        understanding of the mind?

The Making of Me.

Adam Cowan

Does this world want me?

The true me,
The male me,
The soft me,

The me that questions and challenges the confines of these:
Gender roles,
Expectations,
And Realities.

Can I be me?
Forced down by myself even when no one is watching.

'I' stands for insecure–
The true definition of Adam–
Ironic homage to my namesake...
But feel shame by the same background for the fact
    I feel I need a man, not a woman, for company.

My female body,
An exhausted, weeping temple,
I will no longer choose to hide in.

I want me.
The soft me,
The male me,
The true me.

What does it matter then,
Whether or not the world wants the real me?

Lady Patient

Ciara M. Blecka

"Here's my phone number," my lady patient said, scrawling it down with a pink glitter gel pen on a Hello Kitty greeting card. The card smelled of cotton candy perfume. "Promise you'll call. Tonight." She was so delicate and pixie-like sitting there on the examination table, rocking back and forth, swinging her battered legs. She had been picking at them again out of anxiety and I had prescribed a salve, but I doubted she would use it.

"I'm prescribing Ritalin," I said, trying to avoid the inevitable subject of our awkward friendship, yet still accepting the pink envelope that she had sealed with a kiss from her petite glossed lips. "It should calm you down a bit."

She fiddled with her pretend cell phone. "My boyfriend has been calling me nonstop," she said, flipping her long stringy dirty black hair over one shoulder. "He's a movie star, you know. We met on Instagram."

"Keiko, I'm a little concerned about your thyroid, as well," I said. "It's slightly hyperactive. I want to consider Tapazole."

She didn't reply, but instead chewed numbly on her fingernails. She had bitten them down to the quick, and they were bleeding. She seemed to be shaking with panic. I had never seen a young woman like Keiko before. She was nearly an adult, but she did not have the mentality of an adult. She had the mentality of a much younger woman. Almost like...a child.

I knew I was on the edge of doing the unthinkable with my young lady patient. It was not proper for me to befriend her the way I was. And yet, it seemed I was the only one that could possibly understand her. Keiko did not fit in with the other teenagers in her community. Making friends did not come easily to her. And all she wanted in the world was a friend. All she needed in the world was a friend. I could be that friend.

But it wasn't long before I began to doubt my resolution to be Keiko's friend. She started calling me late in the evenings when I was trying to have dinner with my wife and son. My wife actually answered the phone on occasion.

"Who is this?" Alannah wanted to know. She had the phone propped up between her shoulder and her ear while she was pulling the lasagna out of the oven.

"It's Keiko Jophiel," Keiko explained. "I'm your husband's best friend."

"Best friend? Oh, really?" My wife gave me that look and handed me the phone.

"I can't talk, Keiko," I told her over and over. "We're having dinner."

When she realized she could rarely reach me at home, she began making more appointments to see me in the office. Imaginary illnesses began to abound. She started having mysterious fainting spells that seemed to have no discernable cause. No one ever saw her faint, but she had elaborate stories of her near-death experiences, and her mother seemed more than willing to chauffeur her to the clinic whenever she complained of any ache or pain. Keiko was adopted from Japan, and her parents were always so concerned for looking good, but rarely ever truly concerned about Keiko as she wasn't a child of their flesh and blood.

"It may be your thyroid," I decided. "I'm going to start you on the Tapazole."

"Can I take a picture of us together, Earl?" Keiko wanted to know. "I want to show my cousins how handsome you are."

I tried to laugh the whole thing off. "I am old enough to be your father, Keiko. You don't want a photo with me." I had to be more careful. I didn't want her parents suing me for malpractice. After all, they didn't want her anywhere near any men. They didn't want her to be taken advantage of. I didn't blame them.

In fact, it was that photo that pushed her parents over the edge. Keiko cherished that photo and showed it off to everyone, everywhere she went. She put that photo as the background on her iPad. And thus, she ended up getting in a knockdown drag-out fight with her mother over her new-found love for me. I had no idea. That was until she showed up at my doorstep with a package of menstrual pads in one arm and a duffel bag of clothes in the other.

"I need a place to stay," she said.

"What?" I was incredulous.

"My mom kicked me out," she explained. She shifted back and forth on her feet nervously. Keiko always seemed like she was on high alert, her narrow dark eyes darting around her like a little sheep wary of a wolf in her midst.

"You can't stay here, Keiko," I said gently. "I'm your doctor, not your father."

"But I love you!" she objected, pouting out her thin lips. "We were meant to be together. It is our destiny. Unmei."

"Perhaps it was our destiny to meet, Keiko, but for another reason. However, I am happily married and I cannot have a relationship with you, romantic or otherwise."

Alannah joined me at the door, gazing down at the pathetic downtrodden wretch that had come calling at our doorstep. She knew why Keiko was here, but she merely smiled warmly. "There's cookies and milk inside. If you're hungry," she said.

The comfort food did something to console her. And she perked up sitting by the fireplace wrapped in a woolen blanket sitting in my own wooden rocking chair while my wife read to her from a book of Grimm's Fairytales. I suppose Keiko's fairytale life had been rather grim in fact. But, I knew how to turn it into something a bit more Mother Goose.

I called my son down from his room upstairs. Clark was a bit younger than Keiko, but he was someone she might be able to call a friend. Clark had Down Syndrome, though he was very high functioning, and one of the most caring and polite boys I had ever had the pleasure of knowing.

"He takes after his old man," I told Keiko. "Handsome and bright."

"He's lovely," Keiko said, reaching out her pale thin chewed fingers to grasp Clark's ruddy thick stubby ones.

"You're pretty," Clark told her. In fact, she was.

The two of them became fast friends, and Keiko soon forgot all about me and her girlish fantasies. But I had never realized how her childlike mentality was what had given her the wisdom to see the value and beauty in a boy like Clark. Both Keiko and Clark were children who didn't easily make friends. But they had found lifelong friendship in each other.

Hi!, art by Olivier Schopfer

John vs. Mary
(Or What's the Deal with Men and Sex?)

Bernie Silver

John was assistant manager of propaganda, otherwise known as public relations, at Chippy, Inc., a Silicon Valley—you guessed it—chip manufacturer. Mary was secretary to the propaganda manager, John's boss. John joined the company a decade ago, straight out of college. Mary came aboard last year, straight out of a divorce. About a month after her arrival John began pestering—some might call it begging—Mary to go out with him. She resisted until, battle weary, she surrendered. John and Mary enjoyed a relatively congenial dinner at a mid-priced restaurant, then John drove Mary to the home of which she was sole owner thanks to the divorce settlement. Somewhat warily, Mary invited John in for a nightcap. They sat on the couch with their whiskey-and-sodas, not too close and yet not too far apart. After several minutes of idle conversation John scooched closer. Soon he transferred his drink to his right hand and placed his left on Mary's right knee. Her brow creased but she offered no resistance, which John interpreted as permission to climb higher, which he did. In return Mary, almost playfully, slapped John's hand away, then tugged her dress down to its previous nadir just above her knees, while at the same time increasing the distance between her and John. Lastly, she scowled.

"Men," Mary said, the scowl still in place.

"What about us?" John asked offhandedly.

"You're all alike."

John's turn to scowl. "C'mon, you know better'n that."

"I do, huh?"

"Yeah, you do." John sipped his drink. "Now I'll admit that, anatomically, we're all pretty much the same. For example, we all have a—"

"Yes, and that's exactly what I'm getting at." Mary also took a taste. "You've all got one, and that's what you think with."

"Oh come *on*. Certainly a smart woman like you doesn't subscribe to that nonsense."

"It's not nonsense. Of course, a smart man like you realizes I don't mean that men *literally* think with their peckers. What I'm saying is that when it comes to sex, they park their brains and put their most prized possession in gear."

"And what the hell does *that* mean?"

"Okay, I can see you're not big on metaphors, so let me put it another way." Mary paused to swallow more of her drink. "It means men are interested in one thing and one thing only, especially on a date."

Mary smiled, or sneered. John wasn't sure which. Still he risked widening the rift between them despite its possible effect on his objective for the evening. "Any other cliches you'd care to throw my way?" He followed this with a definite smirk.

"No, that one'll do for now," Mary said. "And before you dismiss out of hand what I just said, don't forget that, shopworn though they may be, many cliches are statements of fact."

"And what about statements that aren't factual, and yet get repeated ad infinitum. I believe they're called myths."

"Call it what you will, what I said is true."

Girding his loins, John put his drink down on the coffee table fronting the couch. "The hell it's true, not even close. We men are interested in quite a few things besides sex, like our work, the stock market, sports, good food, and not least of all, tying one on . . . couldn't resist that last one. And it almost goes without saying that married men are interested in their families. Plus . . . plus . . ."

"Don't strain yourself, you'll get a hernia." Mary also set her drink down. "But again, you're missing the point. The number *one* thing on men's minds is—guess what?"

"I suppose you're gonna say sex."

"I'm going to say it because it's true."

"No, it's not. It's a myth."

"No it isn't. It's the truth."

John shook his head, and rather vigorously at that. "No way is it—"

"Okay, okay. Let's call off the tennis match and get down to cases." Mary started to cross her legs, but then thought better of the idea. "What're you thinking about right now, this very minute?" she asked.

John shrugged. "Nothing in particular. No wait, I'm listening to you, so I'm thinking about what you're saying."

"Bull. Setting aside the fact that a few minutes ago your hand crawled halfway up my leg, you've been staring at my tits throughout this conversation. Now tell me you're not thinking about sex."

"I . . . I . . . I haven't been staring at them. I've just, you know, glanced at 'em once in a while."

"Once in a *while?* You haven't taken your eyes off my boobs all evening."

"You're exaggerating."

"Not by much."

"They're very nice, by the way."

"Don't change the subject."

"And what exactly would that be?"

"Don't play dumb with me. You know damn well what the topic of this conversation is."

"Oh, right. Your stupid claim that men think with their weenies."

"Metaphorically speaking.

"Right, metaphorically speaking.

"And my claim isn't stupid, nor is it false. You gaping at my chest all night only proves my point."

"Seriously? All that proves, really, is I admire a good rack."

Mary winced, then informed John, "Flattery will get you nowhere."

"That's where you're wrong—again. It usually gets me anywhere I want to go."

"No doubt, if by that you mean into bed with airheads who fall for that kind of crap. Which brings us back to the subject at hand."

"Which is . . . refresh my memory."

"Which is that most men are obsessed with sex, which causes them to think with their peters instead of their brains."

"I still say that's horse manure. We're not obsessed with sex. We're just very fond of it. And so are women, by the way, which you can't possibly deny."

"And I don't. Sure we women like sex, but we're not consumed by it the way men are."

"Oh for God's sake, how do you even *know* that men are, as you put it, consumed with sex? You a mindreader or something?"

"It doesn't take a mindreader to know that men have sex on the brain. It just takes observation."

"Oh? And what exactly have you observed?"

"Well, you asked so I'll tell you. I've observed that men lie, cheat and practically steal to get a woman into bed. And I've observed that most porn-site visitors and so-called adult-store customers are men. Plus I've observed that it's mainly men who patronize sex peddlers, aka prostitutes, both male and female. This tells me men are so obsessed with sex they're even willing to pay for it if their other ploys fail."

John shook his head, not quite as vigorously as last time, then began to respond. He got as far as "But" before Mary held up a hand signaling him to stop. "Hold on, I'm not finished," she informed him. "Of course, I've also observed men's wandering eyes—you know what I'm taking about. When they're not getting their rocks off in bed men openly gawk at women's body parts, such as their butts, even when their wives or girl-friends are present. And needless to say, but for the record, men are forever ogling women's . . . ahem . . . racks."

"*Now* are you finished?"

"Almost. I've saved the best part for last. I know that some men like to play with dolls, meaning blow-up sex dolls that come equipped with female genitalia, which if you ask me is beyond creepy. How do I know this about men? Some of them have confessed their . . . shall we say . . . affairs to me, and without any coaxing on my part." After a brief pause, Mary said, "Now I'm finished."

John quaffed more whiskey while pondering her words, then offered a rejoinder. "Well, as I said, men are fond of sex, *maybe* a little more than women are. And as for the eyeballing, we guys are visual people, so we like to scope out works of art—such as women."

"Oh puh-*leeze*."

"Do you deny it, that men appreciate works of art? Or don't you think women qualify?"

"What I think is, you're full of it."

"Hmmm. Seems to me we've reached an impasse."

"It certainly looks that way."

"Well, now that *that's* over with, I don't suppose there's any chance . .

.

I mean, I know this is only our first date but—"

"Are you *kidding* me? After the discussion we just had? Now I'm think-ing you're right after all. Men don't have sex on the brain, because in order to have sex on the brain you have to have a brain. But maybe that's unfair. Maybe it's only you who's brainless, not your entire gender. But thanks for the stimulating evening." Mary stood, as did John, though he did so with some hesitation. "Now beat it," Mary said. "And I don't mean that thing you're so proud of."

At first John looked perplexed, but then caught her meaning and did as requested.

Meaning he departed.

3 5 7 love poem

John ("Jake") Cosmos Aller

Missing you missing me
Dreaming about you, do you dream the same
Will love you until end of time; will you remember me then?

If you've been around

John ("Jake") Cosmos Aller

If you've been around
As much as I have
Decades of memories
Fill up your brain's hard drive

Remembering the dead
Misremembering the living
Seeing the past fly past
Everywhere you go

Thinking about things
You did and did not do
As your life begins to fade
Sinking into lost worlds past

Seeing the ghosts
Of all you knew
Whispering Soon you will
Be joining us

Under the Bridge

Allan Onik

Nellie stood under the Greyshot Arch and took a drag of Mary Jane. His rags smelt damp and musty and the Central Park twilight made him reminisce his love for the city. Cindy joined him with her grocery bags full of empty bottles and balding pit bull. She sat down next to him on the bench and smelled the earthy plant smells.

"I've got news," she said. The herb was a dancing carnival in his soul.

"What news?" Nel asked, looking up at the arch.

"Chopper died. OD. Cops found him near The Carousel. I took his candy."

"No shit."

A pigeon landed near the brush and pecked at some seeds, then fluttered and flew away.

The Homeless King took a bite of Royal Osetra Caviar. The Mayor had a taste of some Golden Imperial. Outside Le Bernardin Manhattan was bustling with the usual splendor.

"I called you here for a reason," The Mayor said, washing down the caviar with a sip of Pinot Noir. "Why are you doing this to our city? I know you hold strong ties to the nightly anarchy. These protests must stop. When can we find peace?"

The Homeless King smiled. His rags smelled like sewage and he wore a golden rosary around his neck. "There are some who feel that peace may be a mirage. Healing a fantasy. If I told you and The President that the protests could end tonight what would that solve? A wound that festers doesn't heal. An eagle that is blind doesn't see."

"What do you want?" The Mayor asked. "It can be yours."

Light shone through the draperies and onto The King's face. He sighed. "All who carry an NYPD badge must put down their Glock 19s. They must now use wooden batons. Also, I want an apology written in blue spray paint in front of the Charging Bull."

In the Oval Office the Attorney General dropped a note on The President's desk. "It's over," he said.

The President took two puffs from his Cuban. "Splendid."

Ash took a sip of Jim Bean and watched the rats eat from the wrappers near the dumpster. The morning in Cortlandt Alley was colder than the middle of the night, and his blanket smelled like urine. Chelsy crawled next to him in the crisp air.

"Did you hear?" she asked.

"Hear what?"

"The new Palace is open. And we are welcome. Here, follow me." The two ran through the alley, past the streetlights and into the lush green fields. The Palace was large, jeweled, golden, and glowing. They ran up the golden steps and into the surrounding streets, near the golden barked fruit trees and talented bards playing flutes and mandolins. "Let's go inside!" she cried. And through the golden doors they went.

Give and Take

Don Tassone

"Bill, I hate these forced ratings," Diana said. "You know it's especially tough this year, since we've eliminated two director positions."

"That does make it tough," he said.

"I've got the option for only one one-rating and three two-ratings," she said.

"And one three-rating," he added.

"That's right," she said. "Bill, this is hard, but given two of your three big initiatives this year fell short of their objectives, I have no choice but to rate you a three. I'm sorry."

Bill looked at Diana. In that moment, he saw her not as his boss, but as an intern in his group nearly 20 years earlier. Since then, he'd been Diana's biggest advocate within CPG.

"I'm sorry too," Bill said.

He looked calm, but inside Bill was dying. He had dedicated his life to this company. Over nearly 30 years, he had helped develop its biggest breakthrough products, and he'd personally hired and coached more than half the people now working in R&D.

But Bill also had several strikes against him.

First, he was not very ambitious. He had been a director for nearly 20 years. Now he was the oldest and most expensive R&D director in the company.

Second, he routinely devoted at least half his time to developing people. Now CPG's leaders were judged mainly on their short-term business results.

Third, over the past couple of years, Bill's biggest initiatives hadn't reached their objectives.

Bill was in charge of R&D for the company's paper goods business, its biggest division. Paper goods had suffered two bad years in a row, and people had begun pointing fingers at R&D.

Now, faced with a three-rating for the first time in his career, Bill felt humiliated.

"I think we should talk about what this means for your path ahead," Diana said.

"Yes," he said. "I guess we should."

She stood up, folded her arms and began pacing.

"First," she said, "let's talk about your options."

"Options" was a loaded word at CPG, especially when it came to career discussions.

"At this point, I see three options for you, Bill. First, you can stay in your position and try to continue to compete. But if you're two-rated again next year ... Well, as you know, you'd be counseled out."

Counseled out? Bill felt queasy.

"Second, we could try to find you another position in the company."

Hearing Diana say "we" made Bill feel CPG was a club and that his membership was tenuous.

"Third, we could find a way to retire."

"Retire?"

Diana stopped pacing, looked at Bill and smiled.

"Not immediately," she said. "I was thinking over the next few months or so."

"The next few months?"

"Yes. I have a few retirement packages available to me. If we move on this soon, I should be able to get you full retirement benefits."

So that's what this is about, Bill thought. *They're trying to get rid of me.*

Bill had indeed thought about retirement. But he still had kids in college and was hoping to work at least another few years.

"Diana, this is a lot to think about," he said. "If it's okay, I'd like to take some time to think about what you've said and talk it over with a few people."

"That's fine," she said. "How much time do you think you'll need?"

He resented her pushiness.

"I don't know. A week?"

"How about we reconvene in two days?"

He was stunned by her callousness. But he said yes, and they agreed to get back together in two days.

"Thank you," she said, extending her hand.

He stood up, shook her hand and looked into her eyes. He expected to see something warm there, something that reflected an appreciation for all he had done for her, maybe even a tear.

But instead her eyes were cold, and he felt violated.

#

Bill went home that evening and talked with his wife, Karen. He told her everything. She was stunned.

"How could they do this to you?" she blurted out.

She wasn't upset about Bill retiring. She welcomed that. She was upset about the way he had been treated.

"I don't know," Bill said.

"Oh, Bill," she said, embracing him. "I'm sorry."

Over dinner, Bill told Karen he had already decided to retire.

"Good," she said.

"So I guess it's just a matter of when."

"Well, retiring in time for the holidays would be nice."

#

The next morning, Bill called his financial advisor to make an appointment. He knew he had plenty of money. But now he would need to begin drawing it down sooner.

That afternoon, Diana's office called down for Bill. Her secretary said she would like to see him right away.

When Bill got there, Diana was sitting at her desk. She looked dazed. Her face was pale.

"Bill," she said softly. "Please come in and shut the door."

"Is everything okay?" he asked, sitting down.

"No," she said. "I've just talked with Arun and Emily. They're leaving."

Arun and Emily were R&D directors too. Bill had hired both of them.

"Leaving? Why?"

"Better opportunities elsewhere," she said, "and apparently they've not cared much for the way they've been treated around here lately."

Bill knew what this meant. A defection like this could put the business at risk, and it reflected poorly on Diana.

He felt bad for her. At the same time, he knew Diana's tough ways had finally caught up with her. Bill also knew that if he left now, Diana would be toast.

He looked at her face. The chill in her eyes was gone. In its place, he saw pain.

"How can I help?" he said.

"I knew you would ask that," she said with a smile.

They sat together and worked out a new plan. It called for Bill to take on a new role, working to strengthen the entire R&D organization, including helping Diana get the right leadership team in place. Once things were back on track, Bill would retire.

Diana looked greatly relieved, and Bill was happy for her. At the same time, he had to wonder: once R&D was back in good shape, would she honor their agreement or simply cut him loose?

"Diana," he said, "there is one thing I'd like to ask of you."

"What's that?"

"I'd like a three-year guarantee on my assignment and a 25 percent pay increase."

"Are you serious?"

"Yes."

"Well, Bill," she said with a nervous laugh, "I'm game, but I'll need approval."

"I'm trying to finalize my retirement plan," he said. "I'll need your answer in the morning."

She smiled.

"Okay," she said. "In that case, I'll give you my answer now. It's yes."

"Thank you," he said.

"Let me ask you something," she said. "What was your answer going to be, I mean based on our conversation yesterday?"

"I was going to retire."

"But you could have done that just now. Why didn't you?"

Bill leaned in and looked her in the eye.

"Leaders know when to give and when to take," he said. "I needed to see that from you today."

Image 7, photo by Isabel G. de Diego

untitled (biker)

ayaz daryl nielsen

biker festival
seventies rock-n-roll bands
all these long grey beards

Untitled (toasting)

ayaz daryl nielsen

evening bell ringing
from a nearby church steeple
toasting it with scotch

Birthday Suits

Dan French

"Hey, boys. Do you want to meet Lizzy and me down at Stiles Pond and go for a swim?"

Phee called out from the kitchen porch just as Steve, David, and I were walking down from the sheep shed with cans of creosote and paintbrushes in our hands. Phee was my stepmom and mother to my brothers, Steve, age nine and one year younger than me, David, two years younger, and my sister Elizabeth, who was three. We boys had just finished creosoting newly cut fence posts to prevent them from rotting. Tomorrow, we would dig post-holes and put fence posts up around a newly carved-out field to be used as a pasture for our cows and sheep. Our hands and arms were stained with brown splotches that even turpentine didn't clean without at least a few days of scrubbing. Our clothes were filthy from lugging fence posts around.

Steve said to David and me, "We still have time before feeding the animals." Our heads nodded in return. We put the tops back on the creosote cans, wrapped our brushes, and toted them back to the tool shed.

Stiles Pond was big enough that some might call it a lake. We owned a small pondside cabin, about a mile away through the woods by foot, and longer by road. In the middle of August, the water was so warm you could swim for hours.

The three of us changed into our swim trunks and headed up the dirt road from the far end of our farm. Phee and Elizabeth had already left by car. We walked up the road about half a mile, with maple, oak, and a sprinkling of beech trees on either side providing us with shade. We veered right along a small cut-off path that eventually led down a steep hill to our cabin, a spare one-roomer with a small screened-in front porch.

Phee's station wagon was already out in front of the cabin. We could hear Liz's squeals of delight as she splashed in the water. The beachfront was really a dash of sand in our tiny cove. We had hung a rope from an overhanging tree branch for swinging and jumping into the water.

"Well, hi, boys!" called Phee.

We yelled out a chorus of "Hi" as we all dove in one mad pile into the cool water, refreshing and cleansing after a day's work. Sounds of summer filled the air - splashes and screams of delight from other beach-fronts, an ice cream truck at the public beach playing its enticing tune, and rowboat oars and canoe paddles smacking the water. The sun beat down.

Nothing was better.

Phee looked on. She wore a one-piece bathing suit over her lumpy body. After five or ten minutes, she called out, "Let's play a game. Davey, come over here."

David giggled and swam over.

"What's the game?" he said.

"Well, it's a game of dare. I dare you to take off your swim suit and have me hold you up to show everyone out on the pond," she chuckled.

"Why would we do that?" queried David. He frowned in thought.

"Just because…Come on, try it."

"I'd rather swing from the rope and jump into the water."

"Well," said Phee. She had a mischievous look. "First, we're first going to play my game." She grabbed David, tore off his swim trunks, and thrust him up into the air for all to see his eight-year-old, naked body. David wriggled and writhed, to no avail, and after a bit, she let him go, and with a splash, he hit the water.

Phee tossed his swim suit at him, and then said, "See, dear, now wasn't that fun?"

A couple of canoers looked on and laughed at the spectacle. I watched, squirming. I didn't want my ten-year-old weenie and behind being held up naked for all to see. Should I say I had to go pee? Swim out further so she couldn't get me? Wait my turn and grin and bear it? Why did she want to take our swimsuits off and hold us up for the world to see anyway? My mind roiled. I had a pit in my stomach.

Phee saw Steve out of the corner of her eye, turned, and in one swift motion enveloped him in her arms.

"Next!" she exclaimed, as she pulled off his swimsuit amongst thrashing legs. She held her trophy aloft for all to see – Steve in his birthday suit, screaming, "Mom, Mom, what are you doing?"

Relieved it hadn't been me, my body relaxed. Maybe two was enough.

Much faster than I thought she could move, Phee released Steve and grabbed me by my trunks. "Now dearie, it's your turn."

She reached to get my trunks off, but I clasped them with both hands, and pulled up. I hung on tight, embarrassment flooding over me.

"Come on, now, honey, it's just a game," Phee cooed, as she struggled to undo my grip on my swimsuit. "What are you, a spoil sport? See, Davey and Stevie did it, and they liked it."

We were like two alligators thrashing in the pond, but Phee was a lot bigger than me. I called on Thor to help me out, but Phee had gotten my trunks halfway down and kept pulling. I wanted to swing Thor's sledge-hammer, but I didn't have it within my grasp. Instead, I screamed, a crazy, guttural scream from deep down. I don't know where it came from. Phee looked at me funny, and loosened up, just long enough for me to wriggle free, pull up my trunks, and dive into the water. My chest heaved and water got in my lungs because I had forgotten to take in air before I dove in toward deep water where she couldn't get me. I came up spluttering water, ashamed that I had made such a fuss. The canoers were still watching, but they weren't laughing anymore. They just stared.

Phee said, "Well, I don't know what all the fuss is about, it's just a game." Turning to Liz, digging sand with her shovel, Phee said, "Come on, sweetie, let's head back to get dinner ready."

Liz replied, "Why do we have to go so soon?"

"It's almost dinnertime, sweetie. I need to get cooking."

I felt guilty that I had spoiled the fun, but I also stayed in the deep water where I was safe. I should have let everyone see my weenie and behind. But I was glad I hadn't. Steve and Dave didn't seem to mind that the game was over. I looked out; the canoeists had paddled off.

After Phee and Liz left, we had a contest to see who could swing and land in the water the farthest out from shore. Nobody said anything about what happened. It seemed best to leave things alone and get on with it.

I left Steve and Dave playing in the water and headed up to the cabin. Still unnerved by what had happened, I couldn't figure out why.

Antlions lived in a spit of sand beside our cabin. I often watched as an antlion dug a tiny pit in the sand and buried itself at the bottom by flicking sand up and out. Once the antlion concealed itself, it waited for an ant to fall in. I usually snuck up, quiet, so as not to scare them away, and check their pits. I then watched and waited.

Today was different. I wanted immediate action. I forced an unwilling ant into one of the pits. As the ant scrambled up the walls to get out, the antlion flicked sand over the ant. The ant fell back down to the bottom and started the scramble up once more. The antlion flicked more sand to send the ant sliding back down. This desperate cycle repeated, until finally, the ant tired and paused at the bottom. The antlion snatched the ant and dragged it under the sand to devour.

I smiled, even though I felt a bit guilty I had sent an ant to its death. My head cleared. Time to head back. I called out, "Hey you guys, let's go. We better make it back and get the chores done before dinner, or we'll be out working extra afterwards."

The Dog in the Photograph

Jim Woessner

"Remember this?"

The faint yet distinct words seemed disembodied, as if floating, ghostlike down the stairs and into the family room. It was his wife's voice, an invisible projection. And the words found their target lying on the sofa buried in a Swedish crime novel, his long sought weekend relaxation, his prized "me" time. How could he possibly know what he was supposed to remember? It was, however, the first movement in a choreographed ritual he knew well. The next step required him to respond, "Remember what, darling?" The term of endearment tacked on at the end wasn't mandatory but recommended. Nevertheless, he wasn't in the mood. He resented perpetuating the dance, even though he felt powerless to change it. He kept silent and continued reading, knowing there would be consequences for not playing according to the unwritten rules. He did, however, anticipate her next move, a one-word question with a raised accent on the last syllable.

"Honey?" she asked, on time and as predicted, her voice meandering down the stairs.

He knew exactly what the word meant. At this moment she was wondering why he hadn't responded to her first question. She would permit herself to think that perhaps he had gone to the garage or the yard and was out of earshot, even though she suspected he was lying on the sofa ignoring her. Next, he thought, she will come down the stairs, enter the family room, see him lying comfortably while she has been in the attic organizing boxes of memorabilia. And she will say, "Honey, I was calling. Didn't you hear?" The completion of this thought occurred at the exact moment he heard footfalls coming down the stairs and into the family room. He didn't look up, he didn't have to. "Honey," she said, "I was talking to you." Close enough, he thought.

"Sorry," he lied, "I was reading," as if it wasn't obvious. Here we are, he thought, the end of Round One and the beginning of Round Two, which promises to be slightly less predictable.

"Who's this?" she asked.

He had, of course, remained on his back while she stood without making any attempt to show him what she was holding in her hand. The expectation for this part required him to sit up, swivel his legs off the sofa, and make room for her to sit next to him, which he did, albeit reluctantly. Rules are rules, he reminded himself.

"Who's what?" he asked, according to the understood and well-practiced script.

"This," she said, flashing a photograph at him. "This woman."

Not a good sign, he thought. This was the part he hated most – the implied accusation. He said nothing, of course, because she continued to stand and stare at the tightly held photograph. But then after an agonizing moment, she sat heavily on the sofa, let out a labored breath, and handed it to him. The photograph showed a much younger version of him with his arm around the waist of a dark haired woman, both of them smiling, and with a dog, which looked something like a golden retriever, sitting in front of them looking at the camera.

"I don't know," he said. And although it was the truth, he knew instinctively that it was the wrong answer. Not that it mattered, of course, because he also knew that there wasn't a right answer. But in saying that he didn't know, he had also committed himself to "I don't know" for as long as possible. The steps that came after "deny" were "defer," "deflect," and "defend," roughly in that order. Although defend against what, he couldn't be sure at this point.

"Where did you find it?" he asked.

"With your Navy stuff," she said, taking back the photograph.

"That was more than thirty years ago," he protested, "before I knew you."

"Where was it taken?" she asked.

He paused, trying to recall. "I couldn't tell you."

"Whose dog is that?"

"I don't know. I suppose it's hers."

"How can you not remember?"

He shrugged. "Do you remember every person you were ever photographed with?"

"I tend to remember men who had their arms around me," she said.

"One arm."

"One? Two? What does it matter?"

"You're good with things like that," he said. This represented a slight change in strategy. Offer a compliment, even though it probably wouldn't have the desired effect.

"Good with what?" she asked.

"Memory," he said.

"You've got your arm wrapped around this woman. You're beaming like you've just won her at the County Fair. And you haven't a clue who she is?"

At least I tried, he thought.

"It's probably the wife of a friend who's taking the photo," he said defensively.

"She's not wearing a ring."

"You can see that?" he asked. He leaned over to look again.

"She's beautiful, don't you think?"

Oh oh, he thought, a landmine. His brained screamed, it's a trap, don't go there. "Really?" he said, falling headfirst into the hole that she'd dug and lined with sharpened stakes. What to do now that he's wounded? His mind raced. "You sound jealous," he said. That's it, he thought. Try offense. It can't hurt.

"I'm curious," she said. "I mean, you look so happy, the two of you."

Dagger to the heart. He countered, "That's what you look like when someone says 'cheese.' You smile for the camera." Just then, between his words and thoughts, he remembered the dog. Then the woman. In that order. He remembered it had been a short affair, an explosive one. That his best friend had introduced them. That she was incredibly sexy. And that he wished he hadn't remembered, but it was too late. He realized that all he could do now was try to save himself.

"No, darling, it completely escapes me. Haven't a clue. Memory's going, I guess."

The look she gave was the final act. That and her wordless walk back up to the attic.

Crossed,
art by J.
Ray
Paradiso

Walking Home A Year After You Have Died

Victoria Hunter

I shook rain
from my sheepdog locks
and then hardly tossed shells
in long bent grass

Through a high fence
I saw far out there high slices of stone
the high stone had no evidence
it has ever held shiny magic

It was then I remembered us
I remembered us closer than we are now
often close as towels
that hang in a hotel sweet
for a couple just married
and close as the season jars
we kept in a rack and never used

Always we were close as we needed to be
always the both of us
was in a body that can be held
that should be held

I thought then today
we would have been out already
today the rain
would not be a threat

When expressions would claim
it's a problem
we would go on like it wasn't
perhaps talking with our heads up
and hair exposed

Then I thought we'd also be out
among the same living that finds breath
a precious gift
also perhaps that see having movement
as having power

They would be the living
who will show they see us
the way they should

and then I smiled and thought
maybe we'd be out choosing blouses
with no friction getting in
and those fragile
as the feelings of a child
and those with colors
spilling into colors

2 A.M. On A Saturday

Victoria Hunter

Your bottle
of Wild Irish
Rose wine
is a potbelly pig
bleeding in the tender
over-turned dirt

gnats linger near it
like kids do a birthday cake
when it's about to be cut

I am under a blanket
thick as the snow
that was on the steps
left from the blizzard of 1993

I keep light on a page of my diary
I sketch my dirty secrets in it

the ones no rose
I will ever grasp will ever know
and don't ever think
you can make me tell you them

37

now you sit on a landing
a puppet
when it's not danced
by magic

and that maybe have been left
to be just another piece
of my home to study
and to one morning

before my blood reminds me
it also has pain that won't go away

be chosen
to be another thing
I am obsessed with revealing in a poem

Published by Mystical Muse Online Magazine 2020

38

Sitting In The Woods
On A Rainy Holiday

Victoria Hunter

I am off work like most people in America
under a wide canopy of gray rain
chills haunt the air shake me inside

There's a poem beneath me about a war
an image of a boy sitting
at the end of an ash mountain
with his head in a man's hand

Before my sight are the shadows of leaves
and burnt beef pulled from the fire
and my family the war I know too well
long blurred black white

The Wreckage You Left Behind

Victoria Hunter

Yesterday we drifted into the chilly meeting room
at the funeral branches into the sea
We did not whisper about the wreck he left behind
instead of how much he left us all to bury him with
the keys to his house the power of attorney
his passion for wine and memories of his children

Today none of you are really there
you're still ghosts at the table Between us
you look past my father's ashes
like it's your own reflection
I have not yet grasped them stirred
nor have put them on display somewhere special
as a glass case in my dining room

Good Science

James Bates

Social distancing brought us together. It was the seventh week of lockdown and the governor had eased back on state-imposed restrictions about being in public places so I took him up on it. My favorite coffee shop was open for walk-in traffic and take out and I decided to treat myself to a fresh, steaming latte.

It felt good to stroll from my apartment for three blocks through a pleasant springtime morning and even better to open the door to Carl's Coffee and get smacked in the face with that roasted coffee bean aroma. Ah, it had been too long. Almost swooning, I moved into line.

"Hey, buddy!" A zealous manager suddenly appeared, "Six feet, remember?" He pointed to signs on the walls. In my excitement about being out in the world I'd forgotten the six-foot social distancing rule and berated myself for not remembering the drill. Should I make a joke and play my septuagenarian age card with him? No, better not. Why push it?

He pointed to brightly colored orange circles on the floor with "Six Feet" written on them just to make his point, a picture being worth a thousand words, as they said. I got it. Point made.

"Sorry," I said, turning a little red. People were starting to stare. They were also wearing face coverings, something else I'd foolishly neglected to do. Mentally chastising myself, I stepped back quickly and bumped into a tiny woman who squeaked out an "Ouch" when I stepped on her foot. This was getting ridiculous. You'd think after being stuck inside for only seven weeks I'd at least remember how to act in public. But this was pandemic time and things were changing. Still...

I turned to her as I moved back to the required distance, "I'm so sorry. I don't know what's come over me."

Gray hair fluffed out over the collar of her jean jacket put her in the vicinity of my age. I could tell she was smiling because her eyes were twinkling behind her floral mask. "That's okay," she said, then quickly, and thankfully, changed the subject. "Do you live around here?" I was immediately impressed that she didn't get on my case for not wearing a face covering or berate me for clumsily invading her space, not to mention potentially injuring her foot.

"I do. I live just a few blocks over," I said, pointing arbitrarily behind me.

"That's nice," she said. "I'm in town staying with my daughter. I'm from New York City."

"Oh, my goodness, did you fly?" I was shocked. Getting on a plane at a time like this with Covid-19 running rampant seemed like an insane thing to do.

She smiled. "No. Well, yes," she laughed, understanding where I was coming from. "I flew in a few months ago, before the troubles (as she put it) began."

We chatted easily with each other, six feet apart, as the line moved forward. When we got to the counter, I turned to her, "What are you having?" After a brief back-and-forth semi argument, she said, "Well, thank you. I'll have a latte."

Hmm. Same as me. "Two lattes, please." While the coffees were being made, I had an idea. "Say, would you like to join me?" I pointed outside. "It's a nice day. For Minnesota in the springtime, anyway. They've got their tables set up."

"Sure," she said, "that would be lovely."

I paid for our lattes and we took them outdoors. The morning sun was shining brightly warming the day and it felt good to be in the fresh air. We found an empty table, sat six feet apart, and made ourselves comfortable chatting and getting to get to know one another. It turned out we had a lot in common: we both liked to read, go for walks, cook and spend time with our grandchildren.

During a lull in our conversation, I said, "I don't mean to be too forward, but I'm having a wonderful time." She looked at me, raised her mask and took a sip of her latte, then replaced it. She seemed to be waiting for me to continue, so I did, "I was wondering if you'd like to meet again tomorrow." Her non-committal look worried me. I was enjoying being with her and hoped she felt the same way. "Right here. For coffee," I added, just to be clear. Was she interested? She was witty and charming and it had been years since I'll felt so comfortable with a woman. "I'll even pop for a scone."

She eyes crinkled as she laughed, "Well, if that's the case, how could I refuse?"

Whew! Relief flooded over me. "That's great," I grinned. Suddenly, the pandemic was starting to feel not quite so brutal.

"There's only one thing, though," she said, as her daughter pulled up to the curb and beeped the horn.

"What's that?" I asked, standing along with her, wondering if I'd missed something and offended her somehow.

"Could you please wear a mask tomorrow when we get together? I'd appreciate it." She pointed. All around everyone was masked up. "It's good science, you know."

"Absolutely," I said, embarrassed. "I should have known better."

"Good," she said. "I'll see you tomorrow then, same time, same place."

I waved good bye as she got in the car and drove off with her daughter.

One of these days, hopefully, soon, I'll be able to see that smile of hers. In fact, as I began walking back to my apartment, I found myself looking forward more and more to spending time with her. Her name was Sue. Maybe we'll be able to ride out the pandemic together and eventually not have to worry about masks and social distancing. I've got to believe that one of these days the restrictions will be lifted and she'll be able to take her mask off. I'd love to be there when she does. I'll bet her smile is beautiful.

Old lady Collage,
art Kyle Hemmings

Burning Furniture

P. L. Grimaldi

New age, new traditions;
At the sounding of the new year's bell I recognize
that the old family is dying off,
Like hornet's with their stingers gone,
buzzing and moaning without recourse,
So I burn the old furniture.
The old pieces of four lives without meaning,
Grandmother's dresser, uncle's desk,
aunt's favorite kitchen chair, another aunt's mirror,
Consumed by fire new,
I was tired of the wood suffering from its owners,
from dry rot, being unwanted and unrecognizable,
I cremated the furniture.

Ink

P. L. Grimaldi

Like a bottle of ink in the computer age
with no pen to draw from it
The old man mends socks and washes rags
ignoring the rules change,
He writes with his heart instead of head,
His words glide through the night
As saints and hookers wait for a dog's death
The old man's words become frost on the glass.

Tania's Story

Cora Tate

Why did I ever join the army? I qualified to enter university, but so what. Yeah, Dad talked a lot about his days in the military and seemed to have fond memories of those times, but that isn't why I enlisted. The army seemed like a good place to meet a lot of guys. That appealed to me as much as to other girls, but that isn't why either. I guess it seemed like a good job with some adventure but no real danger.

Our peaceful nation never waged war against anybody, so being a soldier didn't seem like a dangerous job. We took our turns doing international peace-keeping assignments with soldiers from other UN countries, of course, but our soldiers never seemed to be anyone's targets. Turns out our personnel did find themselves in some dangerous situations—fortunately, I wasn't there at the time. My two overseas assignments both stationed me many miles from combat zones, and that suited me just fine then and still.

So, why did I enlist? I was popular at high school, so I wasn't compensating or running away from disappointment. I hadn't broken up with a boyfriend or gone through any emotional trauma like that, so why did I run off and sign up to be a soldier. Oh, sure, I had a crush on Mr. Bronson, my math and physics teacher, but I always knew that wasn't going anywhere— he was married, for goodness' sake—so it isn't like I was broken-hearted over him. I wouldn't have joined the military because of that. So, why?

Maybe I just don't know. I usually know why I do things, but maybe this time I don't. Strange, though—that is *so* not like me. I'm more inclined to analyze things to death, including my own actions. I suppose that's why I keep worrying at this question like a dog at a bone. I really want to understand why I did that—even if it's all history now, I want to know why.

Not that I'm complaining—the army did a lot for me. For one thing, they instilled in me a discipline for keeping myself fit, although I probably don't utilize it the way they intended. Still, I'm good about exercising regularly, I've eliminated sugar and artificial ingredients from my diet, and I eat organic food almost exclusively. Also, the army funded two years of tertiary education for me—I had to re-enlist for them to do that, but now I'm half-way to a real degree with an associate's diploma—they call it a degree, but we all know it isn't really—in legal studies. So, no complaints.

But that, of course, isn't why I joined the army, and I really would like to know. I should ask Mr. Bronson—I mean, Jared. He's so intelligent and so good at analyzing things. I don't have a crush on him anymore, but he's still very attractive. He's single now, too. That came as a shock—his wife must be a fool to have left him. He's *very* bright, he's talented, he's nice looking, and he's *so* nice. I ran into him yesterday at the supermarket and couldn't help feeling some of the same desire I'd felt as a schoolgirl. I'm more mature now and didn't jump on him like I wanted to six years ago, but I definitely felt attracted. He's probably the only person I know who's intelligent enough to help me figure out why I joined the army—but that isn't his only attractive trait.

He was—I suppose he still is—such a wonderful teacher, partly because he is so intelligent and knows so much but also because he treated his students as people and not just names in a roll book. Right from the beginning, we could tell he respected us as individuals—he even knew all his students' names before the end of the first week of school—and he obviously liked all of us, or, at least, almost all of us. There are always a few who are nothing but trouble—for their teachers and for other students, and for themselves, for that matter. Mr. Bronson even liked some of them—I remember hearing him tell a couple of naughty boys he liked them but didn't like their behavior.

We almost all liked him, too—all but the few who didn't like anybody. I wasn't the only girl who had a crush on Mr. B., but I'm pretty sure none of the others had the hots for him like I did. Six years of soldiering knocks the crushes out of anybody, but I still like M—I have to remember to call him Jared, 'cause he isn't my teacher anymore. There's more to my feelings than liking him, but I'm feeling confused and not confident I know what I do feel. I must, though—they're *my* feelings, after all.

We talked a long time—although the time went by so quickly, I didn't realize how long we talked until later—at the market and have arranged to go for a hike together tomorrow. I guess I'll get to see how I feel about him then. Maybe I already know. Funny, I always wanted to have time alone with him, and I never could. Now, I'm going to get just what I always wanted, and I'm feeling a little scared about it.

Scared? How ridiculous is that? Scared of what? That he's going to rape me alongside a trail in the woods? That's what I wanted for my last three years in high school. Now, I'm a trained fighter and don't need to worry about that. Not that I would need to worry about that anyway: Mr. Bronson isn't at all like that, he's sweet and kind and considerate. I haven't seen him for five years, but I still know him well enough to feel sure he would never do anything I didn't want him to do.

What *do* I want him to do? Maybe I'm scared he *won't* want me. But, no, he already told me he feels attracted. Maybe I'm afraid of not knowing what I want. That's just weird. I do like to understand my own thoughts and feelings and actions, but surely not knowing couldn't scare me. Maybe I'm afraid I'll feel disappointed, if he can't keep up with me—he *is* several years older, and I'm *very* fit—but so what if he can't. Why should I feel disappointed? Am I thinking that could have implications for other activities a relationship might entail? No pun intended, of course.

Do I feel scared he won't find me as attractive as he gets to know me better? Do I want him so much that his not wanting me would hurt? Mmmmm... yeah, I do, but I don't think that's why I feel scared—or is it? I don't so much feel scared—more nervous, like before a job interview, not that I've had a lot of experience with those. That suggests I'm afraid of disappointing Jared—I remembered!—but that's crazy. I'm still intelligent and a nice person, probably a nicer person than I was when he knew me (not in the way I wanted him to know me, in the Biblical sense, but he was acquainted with me) as a student. Six years in the military have left me no longer a spoiled brat.

Now, I have two things to worry about, two unanswered questions about myself and my feelings and my actions, or maybe three. Most immediately and urgently, what am I worried about? Likewise, what do I want? I've heard guys make jokes about not knowing what women want. Christ! No wonder they don't know what we want—*we* don't know, or at least *I* don't. Then, of course, there's the question about why I joined up, which has bugged me for weeks, months.

If I'm going to go walking with Jared tomorrow, I want to be sharp, so I'd better get some sleep. Maybe my thoughts will crystallize while I sleep, or maybe in the course of the walk. I'll add some to these notes tomorrow evening, if I can.

#

My thoughts and feelings didn't clarify themselves overnight, but I've learned two things in the course of the day: he sure didn't have any trouble keeping up with me, and I want him just as much as I ever did. As for keeping up, I think he might've had more in reserve than I did. Desire, whew, it's still there just as strong, but it doesn't feel the same—I don't feel the same. Well, hell, I'm not the same. I've been a soldier for six years, and I see the world differently. I still feel that desire, but I guess maybe now it's somehow more mature.

When I was sixteen, seventeen, I just wanted to get Mr. Bronson into bed and bounce around all night. Now, I want to get him into bed and start a family. Holy mackerel! Did I just say that!? Is it true? I wonder how he would feel about that—it's one of the few things we didn't talk about today on the mountain. Is that one more thing to worry about? I think we need to spend some serious intimate time together.

Tanya's Story

Janet Kuypers

(tanya's middle name is marie, and her sister's name tasha anna negron. she likes her sister's name, but i told her that her name was nice, too. this is a story tanya made up for me at logan beach cafe. she was eating nachos with salsa. tanya is nine, going on ten.)

this is a story about summer. phil was riding his bike. phil is my brother. (how old is phil?) phil is 17, going on 18 years old. so he was riding his his bike in the park, and it was sunny, and joe-joe, he's my other brother, he shot a bow and arrow at phil's tires. and he hit the tires!!!! and phil got MAD. phil fell over, he hit his arm, but he was okay. so, since phil was mad, he ran after joe-joe, and he caught up to him and threw him on the ground. they started fighting, and my sister tasha came and told them to stop. but they didn't stop, and so she called my dad. dad came came with the belt (ooh! -that's my addition to the story. sorry.) it's really a mexican belt. (what's the difference between a mexican belt and a belt, say, not from mexico? am i asking too many questions?) it really big, and i got hit with it once. (ouch. -that's my addition again. sorry.)

(oh, wait, she had to go get a drink, she was thirsty. making up stories is hard work.)

(okay, she's coming back now.)

(so, what's the end of the story? what happened?)

my brother joe had a black eye, phil gave it to him. so dad came and he hit them. and they stopped fighting then.

(okay, so we got the good-guy/bad guy thing covered, and an action scene, and a resolution. so most stories have a moral, so what's the moral of this story?)

not to fight.

Who We Are Not

Enobong Emmanuel

I looked at the two people across the street with disdain. The priest wearing a jean and a metallica T-shirt while the young girl wore a tank top on a miniskirt. I eyed them suspiciously. A proper pious, devout priest wouldn't wear such a thing not alone found in the dead of the night with a maiden. But father Francis wasn't your normal kind of priest. He was everything you wouldn't want a priest to be. Even though he had an even temperament and the kind of warm voice that was easy to get lost in, he was a master of deceit. He'd betrayed those who trusted him, failed those who depended on him, lied and deceived them. From the pulpit he radiated all that was good and holy about the love of God but each time I looked at him, I saw the devil himself with eyes the gray-green of a mist shrouded glen.

He reached behind her nape, catching the thick rope of her braid with his hand, winding the shinning plait around his palm. I scrunched my face in disgust as the sight irritated me, unnerved me. Shadows fell across my face as I watched her get into his car. I gritted my teeth and walked away.

*   *   *   *   *

I sat on the oak chair in the confession room, a small box like a public toilet. I had come for a reason, a journey that would never be finished, not until the priest knew who I was.

"Are you there?" The priest began in a low voice as I shut my eyes, shut out the images and the answering ache in my belly.

"I'm here, father" I shifted my gaze to the statue of virgin Mary, her hands downward, palms open and facing forward. I was once a virgin too.

"You may begin." Irritation tinged his voice .

A resolute smile tipped the corner of my lip as I spoke "Bless me father for I have sinned. It has been weeks since my last confession and these are my sins. I am a pedophile, father. Last week I raped an eight year old, forced myself on her until she was no longer breathing."

I paused waiting for the priest to speak and when he didn't, I continued "You know, I derive happiness from what I do. Are you listening, father?" I whispered

"Ye...yes" He stammered, speaking after a silent moment "Why do you do it?" I heard his voice falter.

Pain and hate raked me, images of my childhood swimming before me, spooling my mind back through the years of abuse in an attempt to recall how it started. Back to the place that haunted my dreams, killed my ambition and chilled family relationship.

*   *   *   *   *

"Daddy, Uncle touch my pee...." Before I could complete the sentence, my head snapped to the right. The loud sound of my father's palm of hand meeting my cheek filled the room as I fell silent.

"You are the devil's child," my father spat out. "Let this be the last time I will hear of such." His face contorted with rage. He worshipped uncle Francis like a god. He was the perfect friend. He never had the "I'm a sex predator" tag hanging on his neck.

*   *   *   *   *

I let out a loud, exaggerated sigh as the priest cleared his throat, snapping me back to the moment.

"Bless me father, for I will sin." My heart faded in my chest, like the moon when it is out during the day. It is there but barely visible. "I have another victim."

"What!" His voice cracked and a moment of silence passed "Another child?"

I laughed as I savored what he must think of me "Yes, another child. I told you, I told you, I can not control the cravings."

"You can still repent from your ways, son?"

"No, father," I snapped. "I have done far too much damage, I can't be saved."

"Son, you...."

"No!" I slipped my hands into my pocket and brought the picture "Won't you ask me who my next victim is? A smirk played on my lips.

"Who?" He asked, confused.

"He is 6 year old, bright and lovely.....but I plan to take that away." I paused and leaned back on the chair "His name is Maxwell."

"Maxwell," He echoed, and I heard the panic in his voice. I knew I had shaken him.

"Yes, Maxwell." I laughed, piercing the dead air. "Your little nephew."

"Alex, is that you?" His voice pitched as realization struck him.

"Yes, Uncle Francis. You got that right, father" I stressed the last word "I'm going to do to him what you did to me."

49

Moonlit Ghosts

Jason Waddle

No wolves heard tonight. The crickets on the outside of the house were the loudest sound. On the inside of the old man's house was the thumping sound of Molly Shield's head being dragged behind her body. Twelve steps to reach the basement's bottom floor. The old man was aged, so he was slower. Left over from Big Al's youth was his strength. Al Travers was still ferociously strong at sixty-six. Big Al...

Al Travers was naturally strong. At fifteen years old he could bench press 555 pounds five times. In high school, Travers was somewhat okay with the guys his age, but not at all with the girls. Never. Al was as ugly as he was strong. His voice was made fun of because he sounded like Elmer Fudd. Along with Al's bad teeth, a foul smell (perhaps from the decaying teeth), Travers stood six foot nine inches by the time he reached twenty years old. After high school he was known as the mangler. Why? He either broke or dislocated fellow wrestling opponent's arms, shoulders, or legs— most likely on purpose. No matter the injury, the opponents were left hurt and Al struggled to hide a smile. The odd giggle gave it away. Finally, coaches kicked him off the team before he got out of his last year of high school—which was a surprise to most folks. Farm life was the destination. The town's folk say Al Travers was not that bright. He was suited for butchering and farm work.

He single-handedly dragged her lifeless body— slowly, but with ease. On the farm, Al was used to slaughtering the defenceless. Even at a young age, being kind only to kill gave Travers an almost sexual satisfaction on the farm. Sadly, there was no difference between Molly Shield and a pig being slaughtered. Not on this night. Molly was Big Al' pig now. He would make her bleed for being so beautiful and he would punish God for making him impotent.

Travers lifted Molly's body onto a slab used for butchering. He stuck his pinky finger in his right ear for a brief moment. It made a window like screech as he twisted his finger about in his ear. Relaxing both hands in his trouser pockets, he hawked up a greenish-yellow flehm and spat in a bucket just below Molly's head. Old man Travers limped over and around to the sink to wash his hands. He was hungry and would need to eat before the dismemberment. He didn't always eat his victims. Al was a picky eater. This one had put up a fight, unlike the others. Al was hurt this time.

The screen door slammed shut. Molly left the diner. She walked slowly to her car. It had been a long 7:30 am to 7:30 pm shift. The moon was visible at 8:00 pm and the car wouldn't start like it had earlier this morning. Molly slammed the car door while getting out–

"Fuck-fuck-fuck...!"

Al was watching from his pickup truck. He got out and approached.

"Mi-mi-miss...e-e-verything ok?"

"Hi! I-ah..."

"She won't s-s-start?"

"uh-no. It's heading to the bone yard," Molly said with a mocking tone.

"Let me looks–huh!"

Al reached for Molly's keys. While lifting up the hood of the car he put the keys in his pocket. Molly came around and asked if he could fix it. She switched between biting her nails and combing her fingers through her long blonde hair.

"One hundred p-p-p-p-percent. I can f-f-fix it, b-b-but the t-tools to f-f-f-fix it are in my g-g-g-garage."

"That's my luck," Molly lipped.

"Tell you what, go back into the diner and I will bring my tow truck to get your car."

Al had talked with a lisp since childhood, but when his mind was clear on something, he could speak more fluently–without the lisp or stuttering.

"Oh, Sir, I really appreciate all this and I will pay you. I can't go back in there because my ex-boyfriend is in there. He's kind of stalking me."

"I completely understand, Molly. You are safer with me, then."

"Thanks Mister–thank you so much. How much do I owe you?"

"Call me, Al"

"Sorry. How much can I pay you for your trouble, Al?"

"Let's say you pay for some gas and it doesn't have to be today, d-d-d-dear."

"Thank you, Mister...I mean Al."

"Don't mention it. Hop in the truck."

"Oh shit, my keys!"

"I handed them back," Al reassured.

"There's another problem I've created," Molly gasped.

Molly got inside the red Chevy. Big Al opened the truck door but halted to get in when–

"MOLLY–GET BACK HERE."

"Stay here, dear," Al Warned.

"Okay."

Molly's ex-boyfriend Jeff was big at six foot four, but Al made him look tiny. It lasted all of eight seconds. Al had crushed the boy's hand. The sound of eggshells breaking and the boy's yelp gave Travers a calm feeling. The kid ran for his truck and took off without getting his friends in the diner. Al and Molly drove off in the Chevy in the opposite direction.

It was now dark. Between the two was an awkward feeling of safety. Molly was relieved and surprised that her ex-boyfriend listened to Al. She didn't see what had happened.

"You must have a way with people, Mr. Travers."

He kept looking forward.

"You just have to know your timing is all!"

Al slammed his right elbow into Molly's temple. She slumped unconscious on to the seat. He reached the farm and parked just outside the garage. There never was a tow truck. There was no intention of helping. Al just had an eye for vulnerable animals. There was no plan to kill Molly until an opportunity presented itself back in the parking lot. He took it. He dragged Molly out of the truck—dragging her to the side of the house which placed them in the middle with the garage on one side. As Molly's body was being scrapped by the rocks and dirt, she woke.

Molly reached for a broken piece of metal.

Big Al leaned forward to unlock the side door.

"YOU FUCK," she yelled while slicing Travers's left hand.

Al failed to let out a cry, but his entire face seemed to collapse. He was near rage, but Molly quickly stabbed his right leg. She couldn't get the metal fragment out of Al's leg. Molly was smacked unconscious, again. Al unclenched his fist and ripped off a piece of his shirt and tied it around his bleeding hand and ripped out the shrapnel from his leg.

"I love a f-f-f-fighter. Fucking…"

Al opened the side door while dragging Molly behind him.

Molly was still laying on the slab. Al had his back turned to her. He was washing his hands in the sink that was five feet away from Molly. All kinds of cutting tools were in place on the wall and spread around the sink area. Al had stopped the bleeding. It was not in too deep. To Molly, it must have felt deeper. What stopped the metal piece from going deeper into Al's leg was the cutting of her own fingers in the process. Al dried his hands and reached for a bone saw. He felt full of confidence. Big Al turned around stunned—

Molly was gone.

"Don't you remember me? You're going to remember me, little Al," giggling.

"W-w-w-where the f-f-fuck are you b-b-b-bitch?"

"Do you stutter in relation to your limp dick, little Al?... More giggling.

"I am going to s-s-skin...I am going to gut you a-a-a-alive..."

"You already did, little Al!"

"S-s-stop calling me l-l-l-l-ittle," Al hollered pathetically.

"Such a big sausage in your pants, yet it's never risen since your mother was alive, or was it your father that excited you, little Al." The giggling got so loud Al covered his ears.

"S-s-s-stop" ...thud! Al lay unconscious.

Al woke up feeling dizzy. He was unclothed and tied up to a rusted harrow. The pain was immense. It was no longer obvious if he was male or female from the mid-section down anymore. Nine wolves approached out of the fog and he knew one must be Molly. The leader of the pack approached. She could communicate with Al with her eyes, but Al could only listen to the wolf. The moon was full and hungry.

"I know you remember me now. You never really needed this body part. We started there, no Al."

The wolf lunged with curious speed and instinct. After a few screams the only sound to hear were the crickets and the howling of wolves. The largest wolf bit off Al's hands.

The top headline for the town's paper reads:

Nine Bodies Recovered at the Travers's Farm. 8 Female and 1 Male. Owner of the property remains missing.

The kaleidoscopic Cabin,
art by H.L. Dowless

Lost

Judi Dettorre

Standing in the parking lot.
Early evening dusk
gathers round me.
Hesitating,
skimming the horizon
from left to right and back again.
A wealth of colors and shapes
row upon row
like a garden.

All the while wondering
where did I park my car?

The weaker gender

Ezewuzie Nkiruka Juliet

Ladies have been treated wrongly
right from genesis.
Dressing indecently shouldn't warrant rape
We don't deserve to be called sluts
We can speak on our sexuality,
act out our sexuality
and also explore our sexuality,
without being called names.
Men act a certain way and they are praised
Ladies act the same and they are shamed
Men sleep with multiple girls
and they are called heroic names.
Ladies sleep with multiple men
and she is labeled a prostitute.
Where is equality when we seek for it?
Where is the constitution when it's needed?
Women's rights are human rights
Problem in the marriage?
Question the lady
The child goes on the wrong path
rebuke the woman.
Where are the men in these situations?
Why are they not attacked?
Why are they not questioned?
Our gender is not synonymous to weak
We have the right to speak up
We have the right to voice our thoughts
In Africa, paying a bride price
doesn't make her your slave.
Mental and physical abuse?
I have the right to sue
Ladies! Speak up
Let the world know of our
existence and opinions

Black lives matter

Ezewuzie Nkiruka Juliet

Bang bang!!! The gun goes
A precious life is lost
Every single day our population reduces
Whatever have we done wrong?
We question ourselves every day
We are citizens yet we do not feel safe
We thought the days of slavery were over
yet we still sleep with our eyes open.
We drive at minimum speed
but the cops still stop us.
We try to exercise to stay healthy
and end up in the mortuary.
To them, nothing we do is ever good enough.
We hustle and strive everyday in our own country
yet we are never appreciated
Everyday we lose one,
but we get stronger
They never succeeded in ending our race
They are not going to win now.
We are blacks
We are strong

Police Brutality

Ezewuzie Nkiruka Juliet

They exist with different names
Police in the US
SARS in Nigeria
Criminals on uniform
playing with the lives of people.
They are meant to protect
but instead they are feared.
They harass and intimidate
They steal and kill
Nobody is safe
We are killed at home
We are killed on the streets
Females are raped
Males are harassed
No more!
We want to feel safe
in our own country.
End police brutality
End SARS
The citizens are tired
The blood shed must stop

Rain Day at the Beach

Richard K. Williams

The sky was low and grey
moisture heavy in the air
thicker than normal; pressing down.

On Folly Beach we all knew
it was merely a matter of time.
When the downpour arrived

it came ahead of media prediction.
Fat heavy drops,
pelting those few on the beach.

On the porch, we sat;
high and dry giggling
at those in bathing suits

holding towels over their heads;
running to escape
the falling water.

Astonishing Ants

Richard K. Williams

It's Spring and the ants are back
little black segmented BB bodies
crawling around my house.

I am amazed by these perennial visitors.
Because they appear magically on surfaces
always in the center, never at the edge.

I can scan the walls and floor
studying their stark white smoothness
declare them devoid of pests.
Then blink my eyes or scarcely
turn my head a second, and
an ant or ants will appear.

In the middle of a wall or the middle of the floor
motionless, antenna slowly scanning back and forth.
I cannot fathom how it suddenly got there.
The only reasonable explanation is,
ants got transporters!

They are beamed into my house
from some futuristic ant farm
orbiting the earth in outer space.
They materialize in search of
other advanced forms of life.
And I squish them with a tissue,
sometimes six at a time.

Back Home

Richard K. Williams

The best way to remember
the reasons you left
is to return.

That place you thought
would not exist
without your presence.

Has moved along, like you
regretless. Imperceptibly
perhaps, better than before.

Don't be surprised
when you realize
how small everything is.

Or how vast the
demographic shift.

And try not to linger
sadly, on those people
left behind, lost forever.

For too much time
spent in the past is
as wasteful as

obsessive anticipation
of the future.
You tend to lose the present
which is where your life exists.

And that place you once
called home is just a half
forgotten dream.

In praise of hate

Richard K. Williams

I've heard it said that hate
is a heavy burden to bear

But I don't think hate
weighs one subatomic particle
more than love

Hate is like a warm woolen blanket
on a hot summer day.
Wrap it around yourself and
roast inside it's scratchy feverish hatefulness

Hate won't fade
like an old photograph.
Or slip through your hands
like so many loose grains of sand

Hate allows you to mentally
transform people
into what you think they are.
Rarely being disappointed
when you find out you're wrong

Best of all, hate allows you
to feel so good
when you finally let it go.
let's see love do that.

untitled (engines)

Jack Galmitz

how can one sleep
the engines of night
grind up the streets

Cathedrals

Joe Chiudina

Bus ride home.

I take the seat in the back across from Cathedral.

When he isn't drinking up a tornado, my uncle christens me a chemically imbalanced Romeo who can't tell the difference between a suicide note and a love letter. All that my uncle thinks about is me with a baby carriage.

I don't fantasize about going to bed with Mona Lisa but she's still a masterpiece. Heck, I don't know what's going on behind Mona's smile. I don't even know if she likes me. That doesn't make her any less of a treasure in my eyes.

I look at Cathedral and I'm lovesick. Cupid doesn't have to shoot me with an arrow. She needs to take my temperature. I watch Cathedral look out at the day. I'm jealous of her reflection.

My heart races so fast that it's in danger of getting a speeding ticket. My soul searches the want ads for a mate with some soul.

I want to tap her on the shoulder as if to test the gates of heaven to see if they're locked. I fumble with the safety switch on my heart.

Bus ride to school.

I share a seat with Cathedral. I don't even know if she's catholic or an atheist or if she's wiccan.

I could impress her. Tell her that the book of revelation revs up my religious views. That the commandments are nothing more than tic-tac's for an old generation. Or that Wiccan gives me a dizzy-spell.

My heart races so fast it practically flatlines and my soul does the limbo. My arm aches from not being able to put it around her.

I squint at her on the off-chance that she isn't as dazzling as the last time I saw her. An excuse not to fall in love with her. An excuse not to have my heart burned. I rise above being a slave to a masterpiece.

No chance. She's got me in her trapper-keeper.

I play Scrabble. The Russian roulette edition. "Your name's Cathedral right? Your name's Cathedral right? Your name's Cathedral right?"

She shouts "Yes!" and I jump and cringe in the same breath. I tell myself: watch yourself or you'll give fate a rope-burn.

Her cell rings. She answers it.

"Hello? Yes. What did he say? You're kidding? You're not kidding. Oh my God! He does? Are you sure? Okay. Bye."

Cathedral hangs up and turns to me and attacks me with a kiss and nearly knocks out my loose tooth.

This is a custom that I've always felt was a poor gesture of love. It looks good on the silver screen but until Cupid claims the director's chair, smooches sound like balloons rubbing against balloons. Excuse me but can you pass the gravy mashed potatoes and meatloaf? With your tongue?

Gag me with a French kiss.

But at this moment we're two lips passing in the dark. And I may be a hypocrite, but I'd give my best friend a black eye to have Cathedral kiss me again.

Bus ride home.

I don't want to give my best friend a black eye. I take the stones from my caved-in kiss and bury him alive. He turns the holy grail into a sippy cup. The New testament into the new testes. Robs my soul of its religion.

My best friend sits next to Cathedral. They couldn't be closer if they were engaged. They hold hands.

I touch a rose and get poison ivy. My heart beats itself up.

I never look at another cathedral again. Not even out of the corner of my heart. I give her the cold shoulder and pray that she gets frost-bite. I don't care if I live without love. I give up Catholicism. I hang Pontius Pilate on the cross to spite God. I give up Atheism. I dig mother earth a grave.

My uncle was right.

I can't tell the difference between a suicide note and a love letter. Cupid isn't a teacher. She drives a hearse and I'm the deceased in the back.

Cathedral gets off the bus. But before she does she drops a folded piece of paper on my seat.

I reach to pick it up. Maybe the frame is prettier than the picture. Maybe I can fall in love with a consolation prize. That is if I don't choke on my pride and the church I've built around my Cathedral.

I don't open it up. I unfold it. I don't read it. I meditate on it I read it ten times. Before I can catch up to it. I begin each line with a Possibility and end each line with a sweet Nothing.

'I didn't kiss you because I like you. I kissed you because I was happy. My girlfriend, Sally had just called. Sally surprised me with the news that Paul Fig wanted to ask me out.

I'm sorry.

I'm not going to end this letter with 'I still want to be friends.' Instead. 'Maybe we'll pass each other in the hall sometime'.

Love Cathedral.

PS

I told my sister that you're a great kisser and she wants to ask you to the homecoming dance'.

I drape a leather jacket over my heart. Call the shots. Swagger with a snicker. Keep the prize in sight. Ignore the prize. Let the prize win me. Let Cathedral's sister ask me to the homecoming dance.

I play hard-to-get with a heart-on.

Maybe the book of love is a bible. Or maybe its jokes for John the Baptist. Whatever the case, next time I'll keep my heart's tongue in check before I allow another cathedral to impale me.

Analeptic Lodestone:
Memory Magnet

August Smith

It's like a magnet attracting a magnet of the same substance:
There's a shirt I wear that's so close
to the shirt my father was wearing
in the picture I lost
of him holding me as an infant.
How quick the inscription of a camera!
Within an eyeblink's time its shuttering captured a latent image,
and when light fell on silver halide emulsion in just such a way,
it formed this picture, center of a crystal lattice
of memories bound each to each by covalent bonding.
It was the only picture I had of my father and his metonymic shirt:
black with silver-paisley
amoebas:
(Cascadilla erosion-engines twin-falling:
suspended waterfalls, or pairs of tears).
Today is one of those days
I feel closer to him,
and I move just like my father did:
tuniced in black and silver-paisley.

$20 on the dresser, sunglasses,
sunlight on mahogany,
Terrier teeth
fixed in the puncture holes of father's forearm,
curses thick-forming
in his embouchure
(he sure played a mean trumpet according to Mom)—
he threw the dog against the wall,
agitated more by surprise than by anger.
Mom jumped up and got him a washcloth, pronto,
held it while Billie Holiday's voice swaddled our family trinity.
I was four years old, and that's the only memory I have
of my father—within months Mom moved downstate
and though I never saw him again,
and the picture is no more,
my memento shirt is the only material covalent extant,
all others in this magnet-chain are mnemonic:
and at the heart, somewhere in there, is my father.

A Coat of Arms

Susie Gharib

He was born with a diamond spoon in his head. He thought the world of himself, so exclusiveness flourished into a leafy sort of grandeur and strong-headedness. He was the most unerring individual that ever existed. The women who did not kneel at his feet were born with a genetic bent for spinsterhood and those who did were disdainfully discarded for possessing no sense of etiquette. He remained a sexual hermit while maintaining a public stature as the grandson of a landlord whose property was confiscated in feudal and religious conflicts. The chapel that bore their coat of arms had been found guilty of fervor that exceeded the permitted limit.

He walked every morning to an office that was not graced with a single client for decades. Nobody figured out what enterprise was his. It just bore the coat of arms that put off many customers with its expensive look. His secretary was an old, retired man who pored over a history book he borrowed from a public library down the road. The office had the hush of a church whose worshippers had given up on God. Mr. Stonecrafts spent the whole morning writing in a personal diary whose leather gave it the look of an accountant's book. He deliberated over every sentence like a judge pondering over a matter of life and death. When the lunch hour came, he emerged from his sluggish writing like an exhausted scientist who had been endeavoring to turn ores into gold and bore a care-eaten physiognomy to the nearest park where he consumed his lunch with no apparent appetite, looking overworked. If a businessman shared his seat, he seized the opportunity to complain about the hectic pace of modern life to which the stranger instantly acquiesced offering his own account of endless tasks. He became a familiar figure to most professionals who frequented the park but no one could venture a conjecture upon the nature of his work.

His sudden demise was as mysterious as his life. Not a single relative was to be found. The grief-stricken secretary had to use that sacred key to inspect the diary for any possible contacts. To his consternation, it was an account of the minutest details of his boss's life. Only the pronoun *they* referred to those with whom he had been in contact. It started with an account of the scars that were inflicted by the inmates of a public school in which he was lodged by a very distant relative who had paid all fees in advance and disappeared from a lonely boy's life. The bullying was mainly psychological and focused on the connotations of his coat of arms. His life at university was no better because despite academic achievements he could not make a single friend. He acquired the epithet 'the crownless king' and found his path strewn with giggles from whoever accidentally crossed his life.

Drenched in tears, the diary was inserted into the coffin by the loyal secretary who paid for the funeral from his meagre pension. Fascinated by the coat of arms, he had volunteered his services after an early retirement from an insurance company and found great pride in serving that remnant of the gentry who was the quintessence of politeness. The keys of the elegant flat and office were given to a trust that claimed its right to the property after its inmate's demise. Mr. Stonecrafts died aged fifty-five with not a single penny in his bank account. The secretary spent the remainder of his life wondering who fed his boss.

bottled

jck hnry

your voice mechanical,
eyes gray.
vision blurs
under damning
rays of an early dawn.

a mirror holds no reflection,
cloven hooves trample mottled skin.
tongues taste of gun metal kisses.
i yearn for a touch, outlawed

in 16 states.

there is no peace in your wickedness,
there is no flair in your truth.
there is no breeze upon which to linger
as skies blossom into life, and stones
rest easy at the bottom of the sea.

breathe

jck hnry

clouds linger in a fat heavy sky,
rain has come & gone,
flowers stretch,
leaves rattle on brittle limbs,
water pools against broken curbs.

a transistor radio screams out daily updates,
people with it, people dying
faster than the lies sounding
from the White House.

i no longer listen.
i no longer watch.
i no longer hear.

today,
the sky is beautiful,
out past barbed wire,
beyond burned out buildings,
over gravesites in public parks.

trees bend and sway,
dip down toward the earth.
birds sing and cry, trade
stories with those that listen.

tomorrow sits waiting
for a simple kiss or touch
as we gaze upon a sky
etched by an incredulous sun.

fall cleaning

jck hnry

nightmares keep me restless.
i find myself
cleaning out closets
in the middle of the night.

pockets of old jackets
hold relics, past glory.
glassine bags

filled with stimulation,
buzzsaw vacations
with a burning radiator
vibe.

forgetful in the moment,
i gaze at my tithings.
morning comes creeping.
another lover begs
forgiveness for crimes
committed
against nature and me.

i put discarded echoes

into familiar black

trash bags.
i tear cobwebs

from corners and
slump against the wall.

when i come out of the closet
i may find my solace,
i may find a moment
to remember dreams left behind.

but that moment remains distant,
trains call on in sorrow,
i cut lines of desperation
to forget who i am.

The Terrible Shopper

Jennifer Shneiderman

This piece first appeared in *Montana Mouthful*'s "Quarantine" issue, Issue 8, October 19, 2020.

Evelyn tried unsuccessfully to hide her displeasure as she combed through the grocery bags. Since she had retired and her husband had passed away, her weekly shopping had been a highlight. Evelyn drove to the shops every week in her immaculate Lexus, her nails polished and, although in her early 80s, her still statuesque figure dressed in jewel-toned silk pantsuits. She called the butcher at the farmer's market by name and she knew to get up bright and early when the best seafood was delivered to the local fish market. Evelyn was very particular about quality produce and she took her time choosing ripe, in-season fruits and vegetables. Generally, she stuck to low-sodium food as she took pills for high blood pressure. She particularly loved going to Costco, scooping up their premium salmon and visiting the sample stands sprinkled throughout the massive store.

With the onslaught of COVID-19, the joy of shopping had been ripped away, and Evelyn suddenly went from lonely widow to shut-in. People over 65, especially those with pre-existing conditions, were advised to stay home. Evelyn's condition fit both of those categories. Now, she was at the mercy of her grandson Bill's anemic attempts at marketing, and she wasn't happy about it.

Evelyn refused to do online shopping because she wouldn't trust the corporations with her credit card number. So, she endured Bill's hurried and bungling attempts at procuring essentials. He frequently bought the wrong size, flavor or brand. He purchased mushy apples, salted crackers and off-brand packages of tortillas. Today, once again, when he dropped off the bags and stood six feet away from her door, Bill gave his grandmother a wry smile and shrugged his shoulders sheepishly. Inwardly, he cringed while she slowly shook her head. Even through her mask, her could sense her distaste and disappointment.

After dropping off his grandmother's groceries, Bill sat in his Prius outside of her house for a while. His stomach churned with resentment at her obvious judgment; he knew he could never meet her standards. Despite that, he was determined to shop for her every week. She didn't know the silence and tension that now shrouded her favorite grocery stores—the furtive movements of the customers, the fear in their eyes when someone got too close with their cart, the stomach drop when seeing the shelves cleared of toilet paper and cleaning products. Long lines, limited product choice, empty shelves and intermittent violence dominated the news. But none of that coverage could quite convey the underlying feeling of strangeness, competition and sense of desperation—the prickling sensation that the fabric of human decency was shredding in front of one's very eyes. If he could help it, she would never experience this. He would rather she think he was just a terrible shopper.

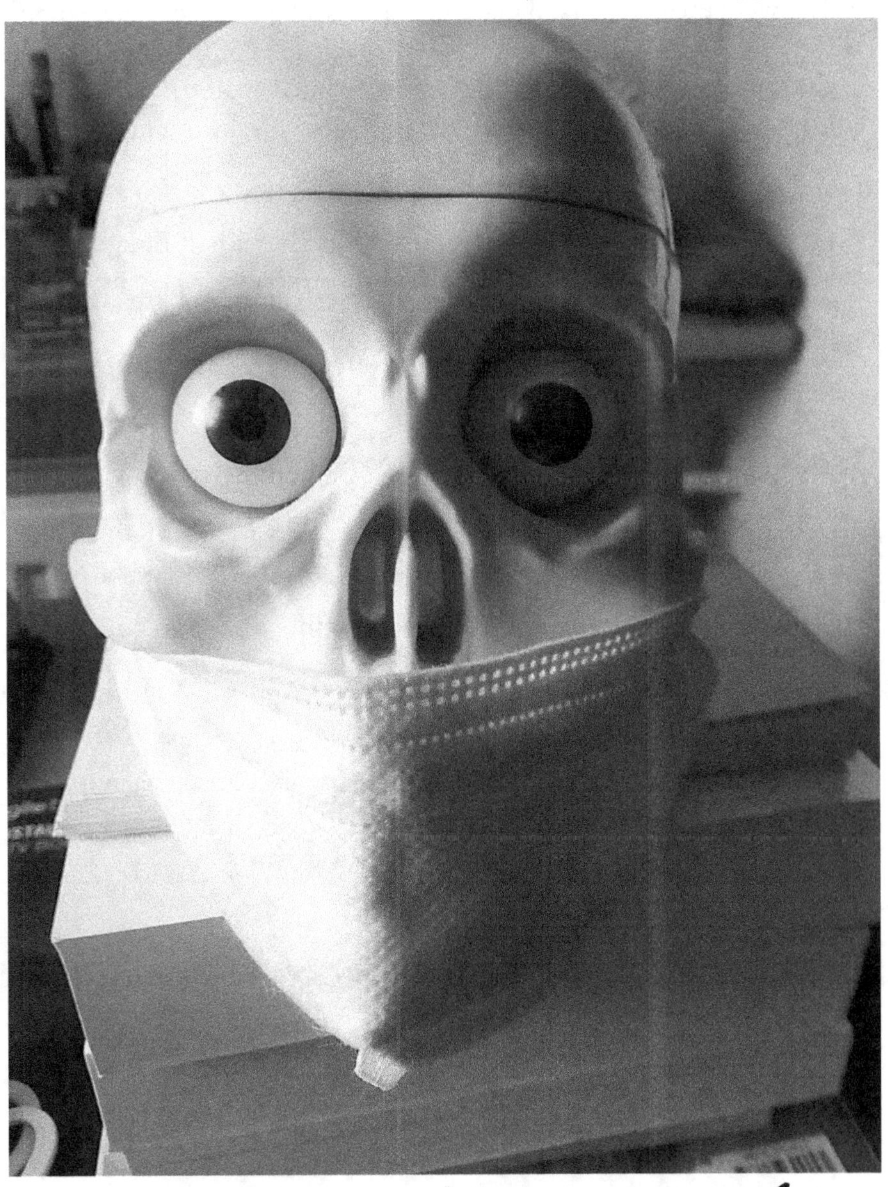

La vacuna Covid no vencerá la muerte, photography by Daniel de Culla

Closed Intervals

Kyle Singh

The wilderness invents phenomena as it is subjected to information.

Cogs project the edges of shadows as braided material.
Deserted windows inhabiting the fog allow masks to engage
     in their own conception.

I cease to offer an olive branch and instead offer a bolt of lightning.
Dissonance allows for a reprieve of wisdom and for glass to install
     itself as the floor.

Engulf yourself in the superposition of events as they
     rotate into existence.
Envisaged by the touch of that which no body knows.

     Knotted strings contrive themselves within you;
        as intestines and as the past.
Pollination comes to employ a defiance embellished in concordance
     with the water cycle.

Toasts are made in the face of connectedness.
Porous rays of sun come to bounce off and align over one another.

Spontaneity encases itself in the shells of hermits.
Curtailed boars state their despondence.

And I come to know you by facing my own knowing.

Cross-contamination allows for closed geometry.
Parallel lines cross on the spheroid.

Unavoidable consequences come from controlling initial conditions.
The spawning of figures comes from the addition of graphs.

Insofar as I know it, the wilderness can not be invented.

The Kite

Sophia Vesely

String six feet long.
Just enough slack
for you to bury me
with the caskets
and still have one hand
grasping the leash.
The other, conveniently privy
to the shadows of these nights.

But on those brilliant, cloudless days,
you erect me in the sky
at the mercy of a dance
I so fiercely despise.

My customary cloth
ripples and undulates
by the command
of your wily fingers.
The sun casts light
and illuminates the red coloring
of my fresh rage.

But I've been watching the ocean swell,
and I can smell the impending rain.
I promise you...
when this hurricane comes,
I will billow and surge
with brazen force.
And your fingers will have nothing left
but a shredded tether.

Prayers and Bullets

Jorge Torrente

El Curita—Little Priest and Nino were intently watching the light armored vehicle's slow approach after it had fired its short-stubbed cannon at the house half a dozen times. They were hiding in the cornfield next to the house and couldn't help but see the big rubber tires biting into the loose ground as the diesel engine growled and spewed out constant black exhaust. Their hearts and minds raced. What could they do to buy time for the rest of the guerrilla outfit to escape the onslaught? The army had surprised them, and this was their last-ditch effort.

The two rebels saw the officer in the turret's hatchway turn around and order the five soldiers walking behind his vehicle to storm the house.

"No one's alive in there," they heard the man say.

As soon as the soldiers left the protection of the tank, Nino and el Curita shot them down and then fired at the officer, but the man had already ducked inside and closed the hatch. The tank turned and came straight at them, its machine gun raking the cornfield with high-caliber bullets.

"The dynamite!" El Curita remembered. "Nino, go get the dynamite in the house. I'll keep them busy." They were lying flat on the ground under the tall corn plants.

"What?" Nino looked up at him.

"Damn it, snap out of it—just go! I'll distract them."

Nino moved instantly, amazed that he could crawl so fast on his belly. With the machine gun bullets whizzing just above his head, Nino headed for the house. The last fifteen yards he ran bent as low as he could.

"Lord God, Heavenly King, Almighty God and Father, we worship you, we give you thanks, we praise you for your glory." After saying these words, el Curita sprang up onto his feet, shot a burst at the advancing tank, disappeared again into the corn, and crawled quickly to another spot. Moments later, little geysers of dirt jumped from the place he'd been.

"Lord Jesus Christ, only Son of the Father; Lord God, Lamb of God, you take away the sin of the world. Have mercy on us; you are seated at the right hand of the Father, receive our prayer." And he repeated the maneuver.

Nino was already inside the kitchen. The floor was covered with plaster debris and fragments of bricks. Several AK-47s were still reclining against one of the walls and a few grenades were inside a small wooden crate. He grabbed two and clipped them to his belt. The other two wooden boxes were filled with dynamite sticks. Everything was covered with a thick layer of dust. Through the big holes in the front wall he could see the tank moving slowly toward the cornfield. *El Curita is out there baiting the tank. I have to hurry.* He snapped up eight sticks of dynamite and tied them snugly together with a piece of the rope they had used to tie up the sacks. He twisted the fuses into a single braid and cut it shorter with his pocket knife.

"For You alone are the Holy One, You alone are the Lord, You alone are the Most High." El Curita stood up again and fired his rifle at the tank. "Jesus Christ, with the Holy Spirit, in the Glory of God the Father! Amen!" He ducked and rolled again. He heard the cannon fire. The shell exploded close by. The shock wave sent him careening over the uneven soil, his flailing arms and legs knocking down corn plants.

Nino picked his way over the rubble littering the living room floor and stood close to one of the big gaps in the wall. He watched the light tank advancing slowly toward the tall corn plants, saw the cannon fire, and the spurts of the machine gun. "My God," he said out loud, "they're gonna kill him!" With trembling hands he lit up the short fuse with his lighter. Then, he ran out of the house through one of the gaps on the wall, carrying his rifle in his left hand and clutching in his right the bundle of dynamite sticks with their braided fuses sparkling angry.

El Curita, dazed by the near miss, felt something wet and warm running down his left side. He patted himself. His hand came up red with blood, and he thanked his Lord for sparing him a little longer, for he knew now that God was with him.

The growl of the tank's diesel engine grew louder as it came closer, but he heard what he thought was someone running close by. Farther away, the unmistakable crack of rifles resonated over communist slogans and foul words. Summoning all his willpower, el Curita sat up and stumbled to his feet. "No, my God, it doesn't hurt," he said, trying to walk. "Don't let it hurt, not now, please God." He was able to catch a glimpse of Nino running at the tank and of the advancing infantry soldiers now shouting even more obscenities and shooting wildly at him as he ran in the open. "My God! They're gonna kill him," he mumbled, and with the last rush of adrenaline left in him, he pushed himself forward and out of the cornfield, shooting his rifle from the hip. "It is me, you motherfuckers! Me, you wanna shoot!" he shouted, as he swiftly replaced the empty magazine and started to sing loudly and with crazy eyes: "Blest be the Lord, blest be the Lord, the God of Mercy, the God who saves. I shall not fear the dark of night nor the arrow that flies by day!" The cannon boomed once more and Angel Valdés y Bravo, better known as el Curita, was blown out of this world.

"Noo!" shouted Nino. Running among bullets, he felt a strong tug on his right leg and fell forward, managing to hurl the dynamite. Nino cursed himself when he saw the bundle land ahead of the tank, not on it.

"Goddamn it! God! How can you do this! El Curita's dead for nothing?" He moaned from the pain in his leg, for his dead friend, for what seemed like his futile action. Frozen to the ground, Nino saw the tank advancing. Finally, it rolled over the dynamite.

"My God, my God!"

The force of the explosion blew the tank into the air and sent Nino flying backward. The vehicle landed on its left side very close to Nino, so close that for a second he thought his fate was sealed. The advancing soldiers stalled and ducked for cover.

"Thank you," he murmured with his head hard against the ground. "Thank you."

The bolt of pain hit him hard again and he ran his right hand over his right leg in an attempt to soothe it. The leg was shattered right under the knee, bones sticking out through the skin. He was bleeding profusely.

"Fuck, and I thought I had tripped on a stone."

The pain was so intense he thought he was going to pass out, but he heard the metallic sound of the tank's top hatch opening. A hand emerged from inside and behind it a human form. It was the officer. The man's eyes were red and teary. "Ah, fresh air," he exclaimed halfway out, and stopped cold when his eyes focused on the barrel of the rifle aimed at his head.

"*¡Hijo de puta!*" Nino garbled from a few feet away, the pain from his leg suddenly muffled by this new shot of adrenaline.

"No!" the officer shouted, scrambling for his sidearm.

Nino pressed the trigger and three slugs turned the officer's right shoulder into pulp. The man cringed but, as he opened his mouth to scream, Nino pulled the trigger again. Holding on and with his jaw clenched, he smashed bullet after bullet into the man's mouth, the bridge of his nose, and his left ear. The hot lead destroyed the officer's lower jaw, his gums, his teeth, and shattered his cervical spine. Somehow, the victim's tongue was uprooted from its base and jammed down through the man's epiglottis, down his larynx, and all the way past the cricoid cartilage, into the trachea, to make sure he would die—if not from the bullets, then from choking on the same tongue that had ordered el Curita's death.

"Oh God!" The pain returned with a wallop. "Can't . . . can't let it . . .

oh, God!" Without letting go of his rifle, he crawled forward with his arms the best he could, leaving a trail of blood on the ground as he went. He unclipped a hand grenade from his belt, pulled the pin, and threw it through the open hatch into the tank, and then the second one for good measure. He heard voices cursing in the tank's bowels; someone shot at him through the hatchway, barely missing.

"Drop your weapon, you son of a bitch!" an arriving soldier ordered.

"Don't shoot him," another soldier shouted. "Let's wait for the Captain!"

Nino looked down at his rifle and stuck the muzzle in his mouth.

"Stop!" the soldiers shouted.

In a split second, Nino's entire life ran in his mind's eye like a reel spinning out of control: drunk father calling him a sissy, the abuse, his mother's dead eyes, the poverty. With all this running in his mind, he looked up at the sky. The celestial vault was painted in marvelous soft pastel colors and, although the soldiers were shouting all around him, he was mesmerized by the wonderful, sweet song of birds unseen, the melody inviting him to fly away with them into the heavens above.

He didn't have time to press the trigger.

The tank exploded a few feet away.

The ball of fire, the shrapnel, and the force of the shockwave killed everything in a one-hundred feet radius. Half of the soldiers perished or were severely maimed. Never before had a single insurgent been so deadly.

His name was Antonio Rodríguez García.

Tiamat and Marduk Share a Beer

Lisa Creech Bledsoe

I am busy not believing we are made of death. I can give up
primordial fear and awe if it means we finally change our story, where

all the statues are men holding guns and slapping the backs
of other soldiers and drinking to redemptive violence, hear hear.

Weather systems, battering rams, shot eight times, eight minutes
hammered home. The way to make it worse, to order and overcome

is to lead the children at gunpoint into the forest and leave
them there. The freezer contains the beer bottle explosion

and for a while everything is still. Except weather systems,
foster care, a thousand other bailouts and news grenades.

The tempest enters her mouth—is choking her in fact.
Rivers spew from her eyes. He is molding the world

from her blood and scraps because that is the story he knows.
But what if we took the guns from all the monuments and

led them out into the forest and left them there for say,
ten generations. Could we then talk, over beers, about why

we are drenched in a legacy of despair? What is happening
in Guatemala, Mississippi, Floyd county? We are each other

83

and the land, ribosomes, North Atlantic Right Whales, not
someone we can hate. The sea monsters aren't who we think

nor are they so easily slain. Not slain at all, right down to
subatomic particles and the Big Bang. And more astonishingly

the dragon doesn't call for our deaths. Let that sink in.
Have we ever received such forgiveness? So much frank possibility

not under our thumbs, our wrest? I'm busy
                    planting mung beans and may be
doing this for the next ten years or more lives than that. It will

tax all our imaginations to see where once love boomed and rolled
before tectonic fractures drained and left us writhing. Who will heal

our self-rejection with dirt, a chaos of weeds, with air
that smells wet and full of blooms?

Come What May

Michael Emeka

A knock came at my door. The gentleness of it told me who it was.

'Mama, it's open.' I pulled on a red T-shirt over the blue denim I was wearing as the door creaked open and my mother's head appeared around its edge.

'*Ebee ka i na-aga*? Where are you going?' Her forehead creased up as she glared at me.

'I'm going out.' I used both of my hands to smooth out the creases on the T-shirt, my eyes fixed on the floor. 'I'm going to see Ikenna, in the next street.'

She waited, saying nothing. She knew I was lying because I always kept my gaze glued to the ground whenever I lied to her as a little boy. As an adult now, I lifted my face and looked straight at her, thinking I could convince her of the veracity of my words.

Her gentle eyes searched my determined ones. 'You know I know you're lying to me.'

Chuckling, I looked away. 'I'm just going out.'

'These are tough times as it is. I hope you won't join the protests.'

'No.' I shook my head, looking up at her. Her lips were pursed in a gesture of displeasure and her eyes slits. 'No, ma,' I repeated, trying to reassure her.

'Just so you know, nothing good will come out of these protests. Our politicians are mulish and wicked. They live in abundance while their people live on less than a dollar a day.' As I made towards the door, she opened it wider. 'Make sure you don't go to protest. They might send soldiers to shoot the protesters, as is the norm in this country.'

'Yes, ma.'

#

In my present mood, I didn't care if the soldiers came, I didn't care if they shot at unarmed protesters. I wanted my voice heard, I wanted to join it to the chorus of the thousands of youths whose ground-shaking chants of 'End SARS!' I could hear even from a mile away. How could I vote you into office and not be able to express my grievance to you when things fall apart around us under your watch? No. We will stand our ground and they must hear our voices, come what may.

Reaching the protest site, which was a popular T-junction, the sight that met my gaze humbled me. A sea of youths stretched in various directions. They punched the air with fisted right hands in unison and bellowed, 'End SARS!' This moved me to tears, for I'd never seen anything like this in Nigeria. The atmosphere was heady, the air pulsating with the collective energy of the thousands of aggrieved citizens gathered. Religious and tribal differences did not exist in this assembly. There were no Christians and no Muslims, no Igbo, Hausa, or Yoruba. We were united by our collective hurt, our suffering, by injustice and poverty.

Tears flowed from my eyes as I lifted my right hand in the air. As much as the tears were for this unprecedented show of unity between my countrymen, they were also for the many lives cut short prematurely, the many lives ruined by the notorious Special Anti-robbery Squad. Some people recognized me and crowded around me. While some of them patted my back and clucked in sympathy, others went as far as asking, 'How did it happen?'

#

Obino swilled his beer, chuckled at the same time to a joke Chime had made and then coughed as some beer went the wrong way. Chime roared with laughter at the other man's misfortune while I gazed in silence as Obino tried to clear his airways.

'So your mother didn't teach you to avoid fooling around while eating or drinking,' I reproached facetiously. I wasn't laughing, but as Obino glanced at me through red, tear-stained eyes, he saw the barely concealed humour in my eyes and smiled.

I pushed back my chair and rose. 'Excuse me.' My bladder was nearly bursting. Wending my way through the ranks of white and coloured plastic tables and chairs occupied by other customers, I made my way to the urinary at the back of the beer parlour. Loud music blaring out of the giant speakers placed at strategic locations in the place tailed me to the urinary and stayed with me until I finished relieving myself.

Breathing a deep sigh, I walked back towards our table and came to a disorderly halt halfway there when I saw the guys were no longer alone.

Standing opposite to Obino and Chime were three rough-looking men, dressed in black T-shirts and pairs of blue denim. Eyes bloodshot and lips black, they gripped their government-issue AK-47 rifles carelessly, looking like a band of ruffians. Printed in front of their black T-shirts were the words: Special Anti-robbery Squad. On their backs were SARS, printed in bold letters.

'What's going on?' I asked.

Chime looked at me. 'They said they want to arrest me, that I'm a robber and a fraudster.'

I chuckled. 'They're joking, right?' I looked at the men as they glowered at us. 'This is a joke, *abi*?'

'We have reliable intelligence your friend here is a criminal,' said the tallest of the men, a dark fellow with cheeks lined with rows of tribal marks that looked like whiskers.

I snorted in derision. 'The only intelligence you have is the one you're seeing with your eyes right now. And that is the fact that Chime wears dreadlocks. That's why you think he's criminal. To you, Nigerian youths wearing stylish hairdos are thieves and fraudsters.'

The men glanced around uncertainly, knowing I was right. But instead of walking away with dignity, they cocked their guns and ordered Chime to get up.

'Up! And out!' they roared, pointing their rifles at him.

Chime rose. 'What's the meaning of this? What did I do?'

'Move out! We're placing you under arrest for armed robbery and fraud.'

'Who did I rob?'

'Move out!' Music screeched to a halt. Noises died in the place as everyone gazed at the unfolding events.

At Chime's reluctance to do as they commanded him, two of the men went and began pushing him out of the place. Obino and I followed tentatively, telling the men to leave him alone.

Outside, a loud bang sounded suddenly. Everyone cringed at the deafening and unexpected *Pop!* I looked around to understand what had happened. And that was when I saw Chime drop like a rag doll, his eyes wide with shock and disbelief. He spasmed and lay still, his blood spreading on the ground.

#

'End SARS! End SARS! End SARS!' Our voices rose in pitch and tempo. Countless fisted hands shot heavenwards each time. The sun was bright and hot, but nobody cared. And when news came through that the state government had imposed a twenty-four-hour curfew on the city, it did not move us.

By seven p.m. when soldiers arrived at the scene, gripping AK-47 rifles instead of riot control gear, we stood our ground, determined that our voices must be heard. Come what may.

The Dogs on Wake Island

Sharon Singleton

It was a hot afternoon early in 1960 when I saw the beautiful dogs in large cages under the scrub bushes on Wake Island. Whining and barking, each was eager for exercise, as any healthy young German shepherd would be if cooped up too long. Wanting a closer look, I headed for the nearest cage. When I was ten feet away, the dog became stone still and fixed its eyes on me. At five feet, he hit the side of his cage full force, teeth bared and growling viciously.

My heart and stomach plummeted, and I jerked to a stop. *"Thank God he's in a cage."*

A young marine tending another dog looked up and said, "He don't like strangers much."

"No kidding!" I gasped. "Where are they going?"

"Vietnam," he said. "We got advisers there that need 'em for protection."

"Protection from what?"

"From the commies. They've been ambushing the advisers. Soon's the planes ready, we'll load 'em up and be on our way." He spoke to the dog, hooked a chain to its collar, and freed it from its cage. As the dog and its handler romped and played, a man approached across the shimmering white road.

"Watch," the marine said as the romp continued.

When the man was about a chain-length away, a single word from the marine instantly transformed the dog from an overgrown puppy into a trained killer that lunged for the newcomer's throat and came up short at the end of the chain. The man's mouth flew open, his eyes bulged wide, and he stumbled backward. It was a demonstration impossible for me to forget.

Wake Island is a tiny coral atoll in the Pacific and a fuel stop for aircraft. Less than three square miles in size, and lying 2400 miles west of Honolulu, it was the layover point for my Pan American Airways crew and me after working a long flight on non-jet aircraft.

After two nights on Wake, we left for Manila, our next layover point. From Manila, we flew to Singapore, with a one-hour transit stop in Saigon. We arrived in Saigon an hour ahead of schedule, and the airport station manager provided us with a car and driver for a trip into the city. I was impressed by its beauty and how it differed from other Asian cities due to its French influence reflected in the city's architecture.

Nowhere did I see a marine or a military dog. Thirty minutes into Saigon and thirty minutes back to the airport was the extent for me of Vietnam at ground level.

Flight schedules made transits through Saigon as little as five days or as long as five months apart. But on my next trip, the station manager's son came aboard to supervise the Vietnamese ground crew workers. Feeling important as an employed twelve-year-old, he was happy to be working and no longer a student.

"There must be an English school here," I said.

"Sure there is," he replied, "but it's closed. The school bus had to go over the same road where a jeep was ambushed last week, so they closed the school. I'd rather work with my dad, anyhow." He assured me he wasn't afraid of any terrorism.

Reading newspapers aboard outbound planes and local English editions during layovers kept me current on world affairs. Although Singapore papers occasionally mentioned it briefly, I didn't find news of Vietnam in papers from home, so I forgot about Vietnam between trips.

Sometimes I worked on MATS flights – Military Air Transport Services flights - planes the military contracted with Pan Am for personnel transport. Usually, they were dull flights with the aircraft crowded to its maximum. But, I picked up one very different series of MATS flights. Bound for an unknown destination somewhere out of Thailand or Clark Field in the Philippines, the men were scared. They told me their mission was urgent and secret, and many feared they would never see home again. After working three legs of the charter, I was sure there was a military crisis somewhere. Based on gleanings from several trips, I guessed Vietnam. I read every newspaper I could get my hands on and found nothing unusual in any of them. I couldn't wait to get back home to San Francisco and learn what was going on.

"What happened in Vietnam?" I asked my roommates as soon as I walked through the apartment door. A student, a nurse, and a teacher, they prided themselves on keeping up on world events.

"Vietnam?" they responded. "Where's that?"

"It's part of Indochina, south of China, the Malay Peninsula. Saigon is the capital."

"Oh, yes. The French lost part of it around the mid-'50s. We haven't heard anything lately, though."

"That's strange. No news out there either."

"Why? What happened?"

"I don't know, but we've been flying military personnel out there for months, and we just took out several planes full of guys who were scared to death."

When the paper bounced off the door over the next several days, I grabbed it and searched for a clue. Just as my roommates had said, nothing! In fact, it was nearly two years before any significant items concerning Americans in Vietnam crept in for public knowledge.

The years have passed, and I've learned the "commies" were the Viet Cong, the Cong, or Charlie. It's hard to believe there was a time when I heard someone ask, "Where is Vietnam?" The ultimate hell of Vietnam's escalation from economic aid to military aid and finally to thousands of Americans dying in combat became threadbare news.

At home, civil disobedience grew from teach-ins to demonstrations, to large scale draft resistance and emigration, making it a war on two fronts.

I tried to console my girlfriend after her fiancé was killed in Vietnam - one of 56,000 Americans to die there.

At the end of a fun-filled Disneyland day, I was depressed by the sight of a group of disabled veterans having a "good time." Scarred, blind, double and triple amputees, paraplegics, some on crutches and others in braces and wheelchairs, they were evidence of the mutilated living victims, 74,000 of whom suffered at least fifty percent disability.

During the Vietnam years, I had two sons of my own. Blond and happy, they were full of the spirit of life. But I worried about their future. Was the stage being readied behind a curtain that would rise on a new theater of war for them when they grew up? Were facts of an imminent new front being omitted from the news or hidden from the public by misleading accounts, as in Vietnam? Should I raise my sons as 'conscientious objectors'? Seek citizenship for them in a traditionally neutral country? Or flee with them to the remotest jungles of the Amazon or the farthest reaches of the Australian outback? Nowhere was there a guarantee of immunity from the horrors of war.

The dogs I saw on Wake Island became the proverbial 'canary in a coal mine' for me, foretelling of deadly times to come, and every time I thought about them, my soul cried for the future of my children.

Vietnam is fading into history, and I have a grandson now. As attention turns to new challenges in the mid-east and elsewhere, I pray my country remembers the ravages of Vietnam and rail against mankind's eternal cycles of war.

Blue Earth County

Zach Murphy

In Blue Earth County, the winters are bitter, but the summers that yield bad crops are even harder to reconcile with.

Mary Anne has the broadest shoulders in all of Southern Minnesota. She wakes up and begins work before dawn even has a chance to introduce itself to the sky. After feeding the chickens, milking the cows, and making sure the tractors are ready to go for the day, she comes back with enough time to make breakfast for her son Rudy.

There's still some sticky spots of raspberry jam on the white kitchen cupboards leftover from the same day that Mary Anne's husband Don got swept away in the big tornado. Don leaving jam on the cupboards when having his morning toast was always her biggest pet peeve. Now she just wishes he was here to do it again.

Rudy rushes down the creaky stairs, rubbing the morning out of his eyes. "Hi mom," he says.

Mary Anne sets a frying pan on the stove. "Hey sleepy."

"I want chocolate for breakfast," Rudy says.

"Eggs it is," Mary Anne says.

After scarfing down his eggs, Rudy washes his plate in the sink and attempts to wipe off the jam spots from the cupboard with a wet rag.

"Wait," Mary Anne says. "I'll take care of that."

"I can do it," says Rudy.

"You need to get ready for school," Mary Anne says. "I'm not letting you miss the bus again."

"Fine," Rudy says as he darts up stairs.

***

Mary Anne and Rudy stroll down the long dirt road toward the bus stop. At the end sits a rusty mailbox where good news doesn't usually arrive.

Mary Anne kisses Rudy on the cheek. "No spitballs or fights today," Mary Anne says.

"Mom?" Rudy asks. "When are you going to clean the kitchen cupboards?"

"I'll clean them whenever my work is done," she says.

Jason Reeds

Harrison Linklater Abbott

I had a head injury when I was nine. It was silly and the first time I was ever knocked out. I was helping my dad with his shed. He was trying to fix the tarmac on the roof and he needed help to hold the tarmac down whilst he nailed it into place. I was perched on the edge. I lifted the tarmac up in one spot, when suddenly a huge spider scurried out from underneath. I screamed and jumped back and fell off the roof. The injury was pretty bad and I still have a scar.

It would be over two decades until I realised that the accident caused me amnesia. And what brought a memory back would be another silly head injury and the second time in my life when I was knocked out. I was walking my dog in the woods. Carla, my dog, suddenly saw a fox and sprinted after it. Whenever my dog sees a fox she just goes crazy. To the point where I have to run after her and bring her back. So this happened again and that day it had been raining for hours. Carla raced off the path after this fox and I sped in pursuit. I ran down a little hillside, slipped on the wet mud, and landed head-first into a tree trunk.

I woke up cluelessly with Carla licking my face. There was blood on my forehead but it wasn't that painful. It wasn't an alarming environment to wake up in – the woodland – and I sat up.

All I could think of was this scenario from my youth. This memory from boyhood which I hadn't thought of in such a long time. It happened here in these very woods:

I was walking along the path and dipped off it into the trees. I'd forgotten my jumper and was looking for it. I heard a noise through the trees and then saw a shape. It was a man. I recognised him. That was Mr Nicolas. The gruff scary neighbour from down the road. I'd never seen him in the woods before. What was he doing here? I crept closer; he was quite far off, doing something in the middle of a circle of holly trees ... He was holding an object and playing around with it. It looked like he was acting to himself, as if rehearsing for a play.

The object was a toy machine gun. I recognised that as well – the gun. It belonged to my friend Jason Reeds. I was mega envious of Jason's gun. All of the boys were and we all wanted it. But why did Mr Nicolas have Jason's gun? Mr Nicolas must have been at least fifty. Here he was, alone in the woods, pretending to be a soldier in a movie. I was terrified of him so I ran away.

I was going to tell my friends. And ask Jason about his gun. I got home and dad was in the garden. He called me and asked me to help him with his shed for a moment ...

All of this came back to me wondrously. I got up dizzily and went back home with Carla. My neighbour was a doctor and friend. I told him I'd been knocked out. He examined me and said I might be a bit concussed but I would be fine. Just sleep and I would be right in the morning. And I tried to sleep, but couldn't. Because I kept thinking about Jason, my old buddy from when I was a kid.

Jason Reeds went missing when he was a nine-year-old boy in the autumn of 1999. And was never found again. It was a disturbing time period and one which I shut off. Because Jason was one of my closest friends and it was never the same after his vanishing. I blocked his memory out.

Now there was this rediscovered memory which could be crucial. It meant something. Did it? I saw that man Nicolas holding Jason's toy gun in the woods, in the same period that Jason went missing. I know it was the same period, because I was in hospital overnight after the shed accident and when I got back in the morning, my friends came to see me at home. They said that Jason was missing and they'd been out looking for him.

Spooky. But how could I trust the memory? Was it even a real memory? The scene seemed so bizarre that it could've been fathomed from the injury. But it sure got me thinking.

Because Mr Nicolas was a strange guy. Nicolas used to stare at us from his windows when we were playing football in the street. He'd shout at us when he drove past us in his van. Swear and holler at us to get off the road. He lived alone in a small house and his big van often lurked on the driveway. We kept playing football near his abode just to annoy him, but we were wary of him at the same time.

I wasn't able to sleep at all because I was thinking about all of this.

I still lived in Mr Nicolas' neighbourhood. He had died five years earlier of cancer. The woods beckoned to me. I thought, maybe, just maybe, this memory might be the key. So I got up in the morning. I took Carla back into the woods.

I dove into the wilderness. It quickly got magical, the ivy heavy and trees thick.

I remembered the place where I saw him. It was by the old trail which was grown over now and rough underfoot. I followed it and came to the circle of holly trees. They were much taller – but there was still that oval of hollies where I'd seen Nicolas in '99. I went into the circle and looked around.

Birdsong trilled in the air. Carla was quiet and hung back. She'd stopped swishing her tail. I looked over the earth. It was winter and the ground was bare and slathered with brown leaves. I noticed that at the end of the area there was a depression. I analysed it from different angles and it was definitely different.

I found a stick and I began digging into this spot. The ground was hard and cold and the stick wasn't much use. But I knew I was close to something. So I went back home to get a spade and came back with it and dug more. It was raining all of this time and the water whipped off my face. Carla was still nervous and reluctant. I worked in a frenzy.

Suddenly a flash of colour came up from the soil. Red. It was a little object with a red dot at the top. Plastic. I reached into the hole and pulled it out. It was Jason's toy machine gun. The red dot was its muzzle. I was surprised that it hadn't degraded more. It was muddy and cold but wasn't broken or anything. I was afraid to keep holding it and I put it down beside the hole. The afternoon was darkening and it would be night within ninety minutes. I used to have nightmares of being left in the woods at night when I was a boy. But I wasn't a boy anymore and I dug on.

I found a new colour. Blue, this time. More plastic, but of a different texture. Blue tarpaulin covered around an oblong shape. I lifted the tarpaulin up with the spade. And I jumped back at the sight. Just like I did with that spider on the shed rooftop. But there was nothing phobic about what I saw this time. It was plain terror, sheer fear. There was a little human skull under the tarpaulin. I was surprised at how little it was. That was Jason Reeds. My throat tightened. I lifted up the rest of the tarpaulin and there was this ample skeleton of a human boy, lain out on the tarpaulin. He looked like he belonged in a museum. I would always wonder why Mr Nicolas buried the plastic gun in the grave with him.

Spit 1,
photography
by Eleanor
Leonne Bennett

Memento Mori

Kevin Brown

My father took the Golden Gloves in '76 and took the bottle in '77. Through outside circumstances and inside make-up, he soon stopped doing one and never stopped doing the other. Now, whenever he was in the bottle, in his mind he was in the ring.

He set up a 90 lb. Everlast heavy bag in the garage. Every night he'd wrap his hands in tattered hand wraps and take a bottle of Jose Cuervo out there. He'd pop the canvas, lifting the bag with each shot. It dropped heavy on its chain and the rafters would groan, dust flaking down around him. The dishes inside rattled. Picture frames cocked on their nails. Sometimes, Mom and I heard him talking to himself. Other times, we heard him crying. He'd come in, stumbling and glazed in sweat. His eyes raw, he'd go to bed without speaking.

Mom never said a word.

One morning, back when girls still had cooties, I woke up and he was sitting on the edge of my bed. It was early, still dark, but I could feel his weight, his presence.

"Dad?"

He sat for a second, not speaking.

Then: "I love you and your mom, you know that," he said. "But I really could've been something."

He shifted. So dark he could have been a ghost.

"38-4-1 amateur record," he said, and I could tell he was crying. "I was the man in the Corps." He sat and swallowed over and over. "Saw Joe Frazier train for the 'Thrilla in Manilla.' Best fighter I ever seen." He exhaled hard. When he spoke, his voice shook. "I had it here," he put his fist to my chin. "Had it and the war took it away." He exhaled hard and rolled his neck. "I was younger than you when I started." He popped his knuckles. "You're already behind," he said. "Time we get to getting."

He opened the door and stood, a silhouette in the hall light. He looked down. "I really could've been something," he said. "In the garage in five minutes." He shut the door and everything went black.

That morning on, he had me working out every day. Before light, when I should be asleep, he had me running two miles. Eating road, he called it. When I should be watching Saturday morning cartoons, he had me hitting the heavy bag 500, 750, 1,000 times with each hand.

Instead of Fruit Loops, my breakfast was 12-20 egg whites. Lunch was grilled chicken breasts. Dinner: salmon and a protein shake. He signed me up for a youth boxing tournament and started pushing harder. Speed bag work, skipping rope, crunches to exhaustion. We'd spar and I'd go to sleep at night, my face knotted and sore. My nose bleeding from so many body shots. Skin burned from the gloves.

"If you can hang with *me*," he said, "you'll destroy *them*." After a while, I could feel myself changing. Getting stronger, faster, balanced. The lungs deeper. The body morphing into a machine.

One morning, a couple of months before the tournament, I stood in the garage, rolling my shoulders to loosen up. He came in carrying a bowl of water and an unopened bottle of vodka. He opened the bottle, hit it hard, and wiped his mouth with the back of his hand. "Better than aspirin," he said, as if to himself.

He set the bowl down.

Biting the cap off a permanent marker, he stepped in front of the bag and squeaked the tip across the canvas. "I'm so glad this day's here," he said. He tossed the marker away, turned, and faced me. Under the Everlast logo, in large capital letters, was:

MEMENTO MORI.

"Strip down to your underwear," he said.

I stared.

"Underwear," he said.

I peeled my clothes off while he strung up two ropes tied into mini nooses from the rafters. He grabbed the bag, tapped his finger under the words and said, "Time to learn what this means."

Outside the wind barreled into the garage door, making the tools on the wall hooks tremble. He stripped off his shirt. Except for a bulging gut, his skin was paper-thin. His shoulders were taut and wide and capped. Every muscle symmetrical. Every fiber and sinew conditioned to perfection.

A long scar that looked like a fossilized centipede wound from below his waistline to the left oblique, rounding off in a tip of purple-puckered flesh. I'd seen the scar my whole life, knew it was from the war, but it was never talked about it.

He cleared his throat. "In the war," he said, "platoon leader told us the one thing that'll get you killed quick is fear of death." He said, "Fear is hesitation. Hesitation is how you lose."

He popped his jaw, rolled his neck side-to-side. "They told us to remember one phrase: *memento mori*—remember you *will* die. Accept it. You don't die in Nam, you'll die of stomach cancer. VC don't snipe you in the jungle, there's a car crash waiting for you somewhere."

He took a long drink.

"One night near Khe Sanh, Charlie bayonet carved me up good." He traced the scar up his side. "But I got him better." He raised one knee in the air, stomped his foot hard, and I jumped. He smiled and said, "Head sounded like a pumpkin dropped from a rooftop." His body was vibrating. "Know why I'm alive and he's not?"

"Stitches?" I said, and his face cinched. He shook his head.

"Fear." He patted the bag. "He had it." He spun it. "I didn't."

He told me that to not be afraid of death, you have to learn how to die. "Learn to die, you're free of fear."

He took a drink and said to grab the loops of ropes. "No matter what," he said, "do not," he told me, "let go."

He took a rag from his back pocket, held it in front of my mouth, and said, "Bite."

My bones felt hollow. Plastic. I almost puked, gagging on the rag, and my heart was swatting my breastbone.

His hand flat, he touched his palm to the surface of the water in the bowl. "Combat's an art," he said, "like making love." He lowered. "And like sex, at the core, it's really only instinct," he said, and slapped my chest. The sound like a hardcover book slammed on a tabletop.

I screamed, bit hard into the rag.

He palmed the water again. Said, "To procreate, our bodies give us the urge to mate."

He popped me in the kidney and I screamed louder.

"To eat, we developed opposable thumbs. What keeps us from crawling on our bellies swiping beetles with our tongues."

He touched his palm to the water.

"To protect ourselves," he said, and slapped my thigh, "we fight."

My eyes were slits of bubbled tears, the light bent in prismatic waves.

"You gotta reach inside," he said, wetting his hand again. "Excavate that instinct." His voice distant, he said it's not buried that deep. Every time someone cuts us off at an intersection and gives you a hateful stare, some of that instinct's unearthed. "Somebody thinks you looked at them wrong and comes at you, they're digging."

He lowered, swung, and caught me in the stomach. My knees went out, but I hung onto the ropes.

"I know this hurts," he said. "Like a motherfuck. But imagine doing this once a day for two months." He dipped his hand in the water and said, "You'll be hard as dug diamond."

All my nerves throbbed against the inside of my skin. All over my body, his blood-pooled handprints.

He swung again, catching me in the floating ribs. The rag dropped, my head hanging forward. Strings of spit stretched from my lips.

And he freed my hands from the ropes and caught me before I dropped. Lifted me in his arms and sat down, holding me in his lap. Slipping in and out of consciousness, I could see the heavy bag rotating to the left:

MORI MEMENTO...

Back right:

...MEMENTO MORI...

And I was proud because I knew he was proud of me. Could feel it seeping from his skin into mine, and I'd never loved him more. "I know it feels like I'm killing you, son," he said, vodka on his breath as he slicked my hair back and kissed the top of my head. "But really," he said, an echo as I went out, "I'm saving your life."

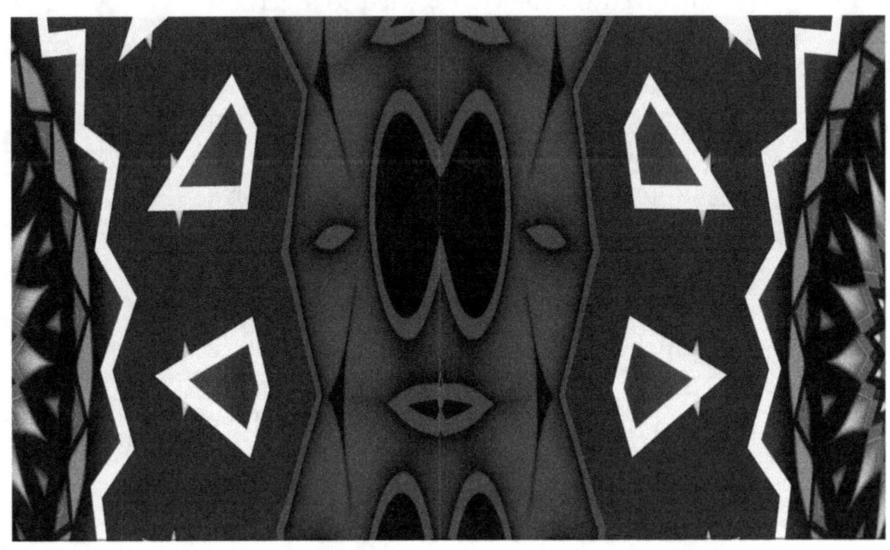

A Daring Plan, art by Edward Michael O'Durr Supranowicz

Zircon, Gemstones, Baubles and Bling

Janet Kuypers

part 1 is dreams 3/13/19, written on National Jewel Day; #NationalJewelDay #JewelDay

today it was like some sort of a contest
some distance had already been traveled
and we still had to get to the last building,
to the back room first, to apparently win

went charging into this strange building
it was the final stop, so I went upstairs
because the back room was the end goal —
but I saw six or seven contenders in front

I thought this meant I lost the contest
but then I saw them all milling around
I stayed on the edges, tried to ascertain
if they went in, or what held them at bay

not learning much, I gathered they waited
for something I know not what, so since
no one was looking toward that elusive
back door, I snuck to it to open it up

once I got inside, I rushed to the back,
touched a large faucet along the back wall
then I turned around and said, "I made it"
and my voice echoed loudly when I won

\#

I didn't know what I'd win in this contest;
my goal all along was to only succeed —
and succeed I did, as I now look back, and
my greedy side now longed for more, indeed

I was invincible after winning this contest
one of the hardest and strongest known
and come to think of it, the word diamond
comes from the Greek word for "invincible"...

"diamonds are a girl's best friend," I heard
a bombshell croon, so maybe today my
award will be diamonds, and jewels that glimmer
and catch the eye, like any winner would

Escaping the Atmosphere
Any Way we Can

Janet Kuypers

After jumping out of an airplane
and watching the Tetons from above,
I wanted John, the man I love,
who was born on March 23rd,
to feel this feeling, like you're
fighting the atmosphere in free fall.
It's like no other feeling in the world.

Then I thought of another man,
also born on March 23rd, who
had dreams of breaking past
that atmosphere altogether,
and in his time, the only way he
could do that was to build rockets
for the SS, and dream of the moon.

It's strange to believe that
Wernher von Braun was a rocket
engineer in Berlin during the
turbulent '30s and '40s, so he
became a part of the SS, and was
the head of Hitler's dream plan
to build the perfect vengeance rocket.

And from what I hear, von Braun
did the work for Nazi Germany,
but he also loftily talked about
sending a rocket to the moon.
'Don't go around talking like that,'
I'm sure they'd say to him, so he
dreamed until the Nazi collapse.

So the States swooped him up
in the budding Cold War, and
von Braun even met with
President Kennedy to cement
their dreams, and then worked
on the Saturn V rocket, & Apollo
manned missions to the moon.

And okay, maybe I only jumped
from an airplane, maybe John
is fighting gravity in a wind tunnel,
and that's no landing in the moon.
But cut us some slack, Wernher
von Braun didn't get to the moon —
but this one man, born on March 23rd,

helped get us all where we are today.

Zucchini Versus Sausage: different choices today

Janet Kuypers

"The greatness of a nation and its moral progress
can be judged by the way its animals are treated."
                                    - Gandhi

I heard of "MeatOut Day" the day before,
and I thought it was a holiday for barbecuing,
and for the masses to be glutenous in
mass-cooking their mass-slaughtered animal.

I'm a vegetarian, & my husband learned
that it was a holiday to eat vegan for the day.
That made me smile, and then he said,
"Well, I guess I won't be eating fish tomorrow" —

which also made me smile. No one spoke
of this quote-unquote holiday in the 7th largest
meat-eating city in the United States (which
may seem surprising, but not in this long horn state),

which means I didn't hear a thing about
this idea of veganism anywhere... which is the same
as every other day of the year. In fact,
while I was out yesterday during "MeatOut" day,

I heard two women talking very loudly
at the table next to me, contemplating what food
to order. Since appetizers were half-off
for Happy Hour, they planned to each order an

appetizer and an entrée (eating there,
I order only one appetizer, and *that* is too much).
When one hefty woman chose salmon
for the appetizer, the other hefty woman was saying

(loud enough for the entire room to hear)
that she couldn't decide between the spinach and
the meat ravioli. So I decided to interject,
and I mentioned that if she's trying to decide,

today happened to be "MeatOut" day,
and when those words left my lips she *instantly*
said no, like eating vegetables was like
contracting a deadly disease. So I smiled and tried

to go back to my work (which was next
to impossible near these two loud-talking women),
but then I *did* hear the indecisive woman
say it might be smart to not get the beef ravioli —

if the other woman's getting salmon
and they're also ordering entrees, the beef
may be too heavy. Okay, but they're
still not getting the *concept* of "MeatOut" day...

so I started to think about "MeatOut"
day being designed to promote our health,
the environment, and animals, and
it was when I was thinking about our health

that I then heard the indecisive fat
woman say that her mother, while in the hospital,
had a heart attack (where she then said,
'and that's the best place to have a heart attack').

The woman then explained that her
mom then had *quadruple* bypass heart surgery.
I looked at the size of this woman,
and okay, it's one thing to be overweight, but

maybe their diet might have something
to do with their health. Crazy idea, I know, as I
hear of men I know taking daily pills
to combat their regular indigestion and heart

burn, and my response is, what is
heart burn? Stop eating so many steaks
and you won't have to medicate
yourself daily to continue eating dead animal.

But that *does* seem to be the American
way, kill as many animals as we can so we can be
as glutenous as we want to be, then
medicate ourselves so we can stay on this cycle.

If we think there is too much violence
in the world, with terrorism and school shootings,
maybe, just maybe, this violence starts
with what we allow the world to slaughter,

so we can injest that violence every
day, at every meal. Wear these skins on your backs
and feel like you have power, when
these capitalists allow others to do the killing

for them. What does *that say* for who
we really are? Brain-washed and overweight
people scoff when I suggest not
eating meat — for *once.* If vegetarians and vegans

get together for one day while
not eating meat, and the people who need it most
won't listen, I don't know what else
to do, non-violently, to spread the word.

What steps can we take to truly make
a difference? I look at my diet, and without trying
I get plenty of protein. But meat markets
convinced the urban Chinese to eat more meat

for protein, though historically they
were never low on protein, but lucky them,
guess what, a lot of them now,
versus before, also have a lot of heart disease.

Listening or corporate cogs
to do what you're told is seldom the solution,
but it seems that people prefer
to not think, especially about the death

they choose to consume every day.
Maybe it's only once people really look at
what they're doing to themselves,
maybe only *then* will the world really change.

You didn't think you
could be ready for this.
You saw a life come and go
and thought you could not cope —

but you're not the first
to battle these demons, because
some who had to face this pain
and strife couldn't even survive.

We all know this feeling;
we all know what it's like.
We know that tension knot
when it feels like everything

is ripping you apart, and the force
is pushing you against that wall
so hard your breath escapes
and you cannot get it back.

I'm here to tell you this:
you can make it. Just pause.
Give it a minute, trust me,
you'll be able to breathe again.

Once you realize that every
aspect of death is still
a part of life, then you
can embrace every single

molecule as a part of life itself.
And then you can embrace
everything, every echo
and vibration, because once

you connect the pieces
together, then you will feel
all the universe's vibrations
as they suddenly come into sync.

Vibrations Echo

Janet Kuypers

Unlocking History, One Asteroid at a Time

Janet Kuypers

3/28/19 (written on the anniversary of the
date Heinrich Wilhelm Matthäus Olbers
discovered the 2nd asteroid, "2 Pallas")

People who love the night sky
also have a special love affair
with anything not from this
planet... I even display a few
catalogued asteroids in clear
display boxes, because these
are what *we* choose to call
precious stones, because...
they are. They unlock Earth's —
& the Solar System's — history.

Looking back, astronauts
believe that is was a massive
asteroid that collided with
the Earth so many years ago,
creating the most giant crater
in the ground and scattering
debris throughout all of the
atmosphere, which killed off
the dinosaurs, and left a thin
layer of Iridium all over Earth.

And on this day over 200
years ago, German astronomer
Heinrich Wilhelm Matthäus Olbers
discovered and named the
2nd asteroid ever found, Pallas —
and back in 1802, they didn't
even know what asteroids were,
so it was counted as a planet,
just like other asteroids found
in the early 19th century.

So back in the day Pallas had a
minor-planet designation, but if
you call it "2 Pallas", you know that
this second asteroid he discovered
(after Ceres) in the Solar System is
one of *the* largest asteroids. And
yeah, 5 years later he discovered
the asteroid Vasta, which is
even *larger* than Pallas. But since
back then the word "asteroid" didn't

exist, these "minor planets" were
called planets. But back then, it was
double-plus cool that Olbers actually
imagined the asteroid belt, as this
magical place all these objects
orbit. So, after all this time, it's
fitting that I keep these little shards
of rocks well-cased and on display.
Because asteroids explain history.
They reveal *more* than this world.

Glacial Ice

Janet Kuypers

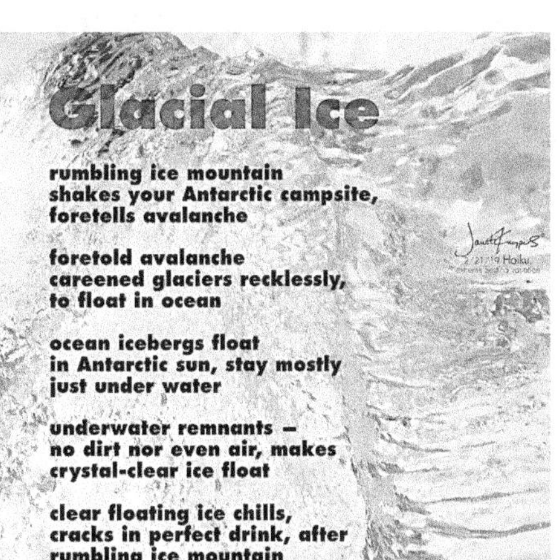

rumbling ice mountain
shakes your Antarctic campsite,
foretells avalanche

foretold avalanche
careened glaciers recklessly,
to float in ocean

ocean icebergs float
in Antarctic sun, stay mostly
just under water

underwater remnants —
no dirt nor even air, makes
crystal-clear ice float

clear floating ice chills,
cracks in perfect drink, after
rumbling ice mountain

http://twitter.com/janetkuypers

http://twitter.com/jkPoetryVine

http://www.facebook.com/janetkuypers

http://www.youtube.com/ccandd96

https://www.pinterest.com/janetkuypers

https://instagram.com/janetkuypers

http://scars.tv/dirt

from the Scars site, also visit

http://scars.tv/books

for a full list of books available from Scars Publications,

http://scars.tv/chapbooks

for a full list of chapbooks available from Scars Publications,

http://scars.tv/art

an extensive Scars Publications photography and art collection,

http://scars.tv/sale

for a full list of books available for sale from Scars Publications